The Gentle Art
Of Caring

People who care for their own lives make the very best care-*givers*. Problem is – most of us don't really know how to provide optimal care for ourselves! In <u>The Gentle Art of Caring</u> Bob Mueller offers us practical, effective ways to enhance the way we think about our daily lives – then change the way we live them! Poignant and humorous stories and the sharing of his own personal struggles to live a joyous and meaningful life make this book both true to life and a pleasure to read. Short, succinct chapters enable the reader to fit this book into *any* busy schedule. It should be read over and over and shared with everyone you love (and those you'd *like* to be able to love)!

- Jane M. Thibault, PhD.
Clinical Gerontologist, Division of Geriatrics
University of Louisville School of Medicine

The Gentle Art of Caring

by

Bob Mueller

To Joyce,

Care and be cared for!

Bob Mueller

PSE Publishing
Louisville, Kentucky

Published and Distributed in the United States by
PSE Publishing
3902 Keal Run Way
Louisville, KY 40241
1-502-640-7811

Printed in the U.S.A.

10 9 8 7 6 5 4 3 2

Library of Congress Control Number: 2003097162
ISBN: 0-9744207-2-7

Cover design by Sue Schaefer
Get Set Graphics

To Kathy,
My loved and loving wife.
Like my favorite gold leaf novel,
Each day, with each new page of life,
We discover the gentle art of caring.

Also by
Bob Mueller

Look Forward Hopefully

ACKNOWLEDGMENTS

Perhaps a man learns almost as much about the gentle art of caring when he fails at intimacy as when he succeeds. I have done both. But this book is dedicated to the people who have been my teachers in success.

First, my many colleagues at Hospice & Palliative Care of Louisville. We are in and out of each other's offices all day long, not merely because we need to talk about the people we serve, but because we need to talk with one another about ourselves. I tell them my daily victories and defeats. I can do this because they do the same with me.

Caring has a way of being intergenerational. Looking in one direction, I am grateful to Elmer and Rita Mueller, from whom I came. Looking in the other direction, all the people I come in contact with from whom I both give love and learn love.

But most of all, this book is for Kathy, who tells me that I am her best friend and who certainly is that to me. It is one of life's happiest gifts that we get to be married to each other. Kathy's gentle art of caring has included endless hours of typesetting, editing, proofreading and simplifying each chapter to make this book more readable.

Thanks to the many people who have encouraged me to publish and to speak: Cathy Zion and Anita Oldham of *Today's Woman* magazine; Rob Patterson of *Reporters, Inc.*; John Hassman owner of A Taste of Kentucky stores; my Rotarian and hospice colleagues; members of Kiwanis, Lions, Optimist, church, retirement and professional women's and men's clubs; and numerous others. Your encouragement has made this book possible.

Finally, a special thanks to my hospice colleague Stephanie Smith who proofread and edited the text and to Kay Johnson who helped with early drafts.

CONTENTS

FOREWORD

Since that day about ten years ago when Bob Mueller called to ask if I might be interested in printing his stories in Today's Woman magazine, we have published more than 80 of his inspirational columns. He doesn't submit his columns at regular intervals, but instead writes when the Spirit moves him, often several stories at a time.

When he sends the stories I save them into a file I have on my laptop computer. The file is simply named "Bob." Over the years, the file has grown quite large. When I click on my "Bob" file, I can scroll down through titles such as "How to Sleep at Night" or "Get a Cause Today" or "Cultivate Yourself." Once I click on a title, a story opens. As I read his thoughts, I find myself thinking differently – thinking beyond where I was...

Reading Bob's stories is like sitting and talking to him -- hearing his thoughts on life and reactions to what he has learned through caring for others. Many of his messages isolate a moment in history - perhaps seeing a person in the best or worst situation that life has to offer -- so that one can ponder its true meaning.

I am happy to see that you now have your own file of stories by Bob. He didn't call this book "Bob" like my file – I see he named it "The Gentle Art of Caring." I think my "Bob" file could be named that too. Caring...we all need more of it. From the thoughts we put into our heads to the words we put into the world, more care could bring more peace to life.

Anita Oldham
Editor, *Today's Woman* magazine

INTRODUCTION

I spent first and second grade growing up in the small Midwestern town of Decatur, Illinois. As I think back, it seems to me we kids had the modern psychologists figured out before our time.

We could tell you in two seconds flat which people in our block had the most "empathy", and we didn't even know there was such a word! There were lots of other things we could tell you right off, too, like which wealthy men in our town loved their money and which loved their families. We knew the spinster ladies who suffered from chronic self-pity and loneliness, and the ones who had rich, full lives, stretching the hours out like rubber bands to encompass church, the sick, the children of their neighborhood, and their gardens.

We could rattle off the names of the good mothers and the not-so-good ones. We had our own rules for deciding. The good ones kissed a hurt away, planned picnics for the family, came away from scrubbing a floor to see the first robin or the first snowman of the season, went to the school play, and smiled with their eyes as well as their mouths when you gave them a fresh-picked bunch of dandelions in the spring.

There were other things we knew, too – such as the screamers and the shouters. "Stay off the clean kitchen floor with those muddy shoes, you brats!" was Mrs. Jumpy. Her husband was "Get off the lawn!" Mrs. Edgy was "For goodness sake, stop all that noise!" We knew the quiet ones, too – the ones who smiled and said, "Maybe you children would like to take your muddy shoes off before you walk across the nice clean floor." Or "How about using the sidewalk, kids, and letting the lawn grow its quarter inch today?"

We knew every cookie jar owner in our part of town – and the kind of cookies in each jar. The cookie ladies were usually the same ones who noticed when we got new roller skates and who took the time to stand on the front porch and cheer us on our first wobbly trip around the block. They were the ones, who noticed new shoes or a missing tooth. When we ran into them at the grocery store, they often said to old Mrs. Jones, "And maybe you'll find a lollipop or two for my little friends here."

By the time we were in first grade we knew the people we could talk to – the ones who understood when a new baby came or when Grandpa died or when Mom had to go to the hospital. They gave us lemonade in the summer and hot chocolate in the winter and listened to our problems and told us cheerful, wonderful things that made us feel much better way inside.

We kids knew the best teachers in our school, too. We wouldn't have understood what "dedicated" meant, but we could point out the ones who smiled when they helped us on with our galoshes and the ones who let us make real homemade valentines in class instead of the kit kind. They were the teachers who really liked our little school and who really liked us. We weren't old enough to understand about the other kind – the ones who were marking time in our school on the way to a better salary, or on the way to the altar, or on the way to their next degree, or who had let circumstances sour their personalities. All we knew was that some teachers made us feel good and made the sun shine even on cloudy days.

I don't suppose we could have understood then, even if we'd been told, that some people are born with a greater talent for caring, just the way some have a greater talent for art or music, while for others it is an asset that must be acquired.

Those who are born with it have a great gift to start with, and those who acquire it are blessed, too, in the very learning. Some learn after a tragedy, or after a period of deep self-appraisal that sets off an almost volcanic eruption. Such an eruption can release a dormant talent for really caring about others, an ability to want to understand them, to take a deep interest in their lives and future.

The Gentle Art of Caring

Today I understand all these things – and I still don't need the psychologists' explanation. I know the people who care, and I still gravitate toward them the way I did back in the town of my first and second grade. I know just which people can give me a lift, can make my day a brighter one, can make me happier for just a few minutes in their company. Always it is the man or woman who knows the gentle art of caring.

The messages in this book are about positive living and the gentle art of caring. Much like my first book, *Look Forward Hopefully*, many of the messages in this book have appeared in *Today's Woman* and *Reporters*.

PART ONE - THINGS THAT GIVE ME STRENGTH

Things That Give Me Strength

For me strength and peace of mind come from several different areas of life. I hope they will do the same for you.

1. **Recognize your mind-sets.** My wife makes me very aware of the mind-sets from which I operate. I used to save everything, especially books. Now my mind-set is to simplify and make room for abundance in my life. I take advantage of the library for my reading needs or donate books that I purchase to various groups. I used to make negative, cynical comments about things. Now my mind-set is to make positive, grateful remarks.

2. **Recall your memories of courage.** When I lack confidence or feel overwhelmed in a situation, I recall times when I exhibited courage. I remember personal success stories that give me strength in the present.

3. **Remember your models, mentors, and spiritual guides.** Over the years there are many people who have inspired me and some who continue to do so. They are guiding spirits I have known. Some have been hospice patients I have visited. Others have been teachers, co-workers, leaders in the non-profit world, and even individuals I have met only once. One priest friend says that his heroes belong to the ages and are always at least over two hundred years old. Historical figures and personalities can be models for all time.

4. **Use your favorite quotes as daily affirmations.** I am a collector of quotes that I refer to as daily affirmations. It's an easy process. There are so many great things said that it's worth taking note. Quotes such as the following:

"It's easy to get good players. Getting them to play together, that's the hard part."
-Casey Stengel

"Everyone's life is a fairy tale written by God's finger."   -Hans Christian Anderson

"Nobody can make you feel inferior without your consent."
-Eleanor Roosevelt

"Love yourself first and everything else falls into line. You really have to love yourself to get anything done in this world."
-Lucille Ball

"An optimist goes to the window every morning and says, 'Good morning, God.' The pessimist goes to the window and says, 'Good God, morning.'"
-Anonymous

5. **Volunteering can take you outside of yourself.** I have volunteered for many different organizations over the years including Hospice & Palliative Care of Louisville, Home of the Innocents, Rotary, and various churches. Each time I do, I receive far more than I give. We have some 400 volunteers at Hospice & Palliative Care of Louisville. They constantly give thanks for being a hospice volunteer because of all they receive from the experience.

6. **Take time for meditation.** So much of life is about hustle and bustle. Every day I take at least ten to thirty minutes to quiet myself and meditate. You can do this in so many ways: transcendental meditation, centering prayer, a walk, sitting quietly in a chair, etc. I need this time to center and to focus. This is more important to me than constant activity. It brings me inner peace, self-confidence, and optimum results.

7. **Get involved with a cause.** My cause is hospice. It's about living and dying. One of our hospice volunteers always says, "With hospice you can be a person's last best friend." It's awesome what we can do during a difficult time in life by just knowing what to do and then taking the time to care and listen. I have received more from patients' last days and words than I have ever given. This is true of so many of the wonderful causes in our world. Find your cause or causes and see what strength this brings.

8. **Use humor.** I always look for the humorous side of life. I am a collector of jokes and am always sending them to various publications. As a fundraiser I find there are many good fundraising jokes. One of my favorites is the one about the preacher who was talking to the church organist. "When I finish my sermon," he said, "I'll ask for all those in the congregation who want to contribute $400 toward the church mortgage to stand up. In the meantime, you provide appropriate music."

   "What do you mean, 'appropriate music'?"

   "Play 'The Star-Spangled Banner.'"

Remember Your Mentors
and Spiritual Guides

In our world of big names and celebrities, our true heroes tend to be anonymous. I can prove this fact with the following test:

- Name the last five years of Academy Award winners for best actor and actress.
- Name the last five years of Super Bowl winners.
- Name the last five winners of *Time* magazine's person of the year.
- Name the last five winners of the Nobel Peace prize.
- Name the last five winners of the Miss America contest.

How did you do? I failed miserably. Here is another test. I bet you do better on this one.

- Name five of your personal heroes who have died.
- Name five friends who have helped you.
- Name several teachers who made a difference in your life.
- Name five co-workers who made you feel special.
- Name five family members or neighbors you admire.

Over the years there are many people who have inspired me. They are guiding spirits I have known. Here are a few of them.

One was an older priest who had poor eyesight plus additional ailments. However, his sense of humor made him an inspiration in observing the lighter side of life. The parish where he was assigned never needed an answering machine because he made his ministry answering the phone. He would frequently pretend he was an answering machine and state: "Masses are at 7:30, 9, 10:30 and noon and funerals on request." Or he would say, "This is a tape that has been programmed to answer 1,001 questions. What's your question?" If he celebrated Mass, he might have trouble seeing a familiar Gospel story like the Good Samaritan. He would stop in the middle of the reading and just say, "Oh, you all know the rest of the story."

If it were not for a seminary teacher in Baltimore, I would probably not be writing these columns today. He is a masterful writer and poet, well published and well known in the Baltimore community. He took the time and caring to encourage me in my writing efforts. He provided all the inspiration I needed.

Every successful non-profit seems to have one person or several persons who are guiding lights for that organization. With countless non-profits I have worked with over the years there are true heroes who are steadfast in their belief for their cause whether it be an inner city day care, an animal shelter, or a hospice. These individuals seek nothing but are motivated by the greatness of their cause. I am always moved by their steadfastness and humility.

Many hospice patients have given me far more than I ever gave them. Often hospice staff and volunteers become a hospice patient's last best friend. These patients share their secrets of living and dying. They pass on their legacy of faith, hope and love to those who stand by their bedside. It is always an uplifting and moving experience.

Who are your models, mentors, and spiritual guides? They might be teachers, co-workers, parents, relatives, or individuals you only met once. It's a terrific exercise to make you appreciate good people in your life. Also think of the people that look up to you as their hero and guide. This is an affirming exercise to realize your importance and value to others.

My Favorite Quotes

I am a collector of quotes that can be used as daily affirmations and guides. There are so many great things said that are noteworthy. Here are some of my favorites ones that center around specific themes.

In the area of letting go and not trying to control everything these quotes are terrific ones:

- *"Never try to teach a pig to sing. It wastes your time and it annoys the pig."*
- *"When it starts to rain, let it."*
- *"Don't push the river. (It flows by itself.)"*
- *"People plan. God laughs!"*

For wisdom I always go to these three quotes:

- *"The art of being wise is the art of knowing what to overlook."* -William James
- *"Wisdom comes by suffering."* -Greek proverb
- *"Who knows not, and knows not that he knows not, is foolish; shun him.*

   Who knows not, and know that he knows not, is humble; teach him.

   Who knows, but knows not that he knows, is asleep; wake him.

   Who knows, and knows that he knows, is wise; follow him."

My favorite friendship quote is:

- *"A friend is someone who can see through you and still enjoys the show."*

At hospice we believe strongly in Jonathan Swift's quote:

- *"May you live all the days of your life."*

The best quotes on change and growth that I've found are these:

- *"If you're green you grow, if you're ripe you rot."*

The Gentle Art of Caring

- *"You have to move up to another level of thinking, which is true for me and everybody else. Everybody has to learn to think differently, bigger, to be open to possibilities."* - Oprah Winfrey

- *"Every noble work is at first impossible."* -Carlyle

- *"When I learn something new – and it happens every day – I feel a little more at home in this universe, a little more comfortable in the nest."* -Bill Moyers

- *"We cannot become what we need to be by remaining what we are."* -Max DePree

Two wonderful quotes on giving are:

- *"A candle loses nothing by lighting another candle."*

- *"There are two ways of spreading light: to be a candle, or the mirror that reflects it."* -Edith Wharton

Quotes that motivate me to action are:

- *"Those who believe that they can do something and those who believe they can't are both right."* -Henry Ford

- *"Anything you may hold firmly in your imagination can be yours."* -William James

- *"You are already enlightened, the only question is: how long will it take you to realize this fact?"* -Krishnamurti

- *"No matter how qualified or deserving we are, we will never reach a better life until we can imagine it for ourselves and allow others to have it."* -Richard Bach

My favorite quote on love is from Julian of Norwich:

- *"We have been loved from before the beginning."*

Two other quotes I love are these:

"When it is dark enough, you can see the stars."

-Ralph Waldo Emerson

"The really great makes you feel that you, too, can become great." -Mark Twain

Start collecting your own quotes. You will find them everywhere. As they become your own, they can inspire you each day to expand your horizons.

The Most Uplifting Work I've Done

"It sure must be depressing to work with the terminally ill!" I could never work for Hospice. It must be a real downer, right?" People make these remarks to me over and over.

My response is always: "No, it's just the opposite. In fact, it's the most uplifting work I've ever done!"

To be with someone with a life-limiting illness is a powerful experience as they face life and death issues. These patients share their life stories. They smile with joy and happiness. They cry with guilt and sadness. They remember and enjoy those close to them. They confront the issues of salvation and life after death. They deny their illness; they bargain with God; they get depressed; and they accept the reality of their condition from day to day.

Hospice care is for the entire household and extended family. Often relatives and friends of hospice patients experience grief and loss before the patient's death. Sometimes they are afraid to communicate with their seriously ill loved one. Frequently they are looking for someone to guide them through the journey.

The word "hospice" means hospitality, a lodging or inn, a place of rest for pilgrims or travelers, for the destitute or sick. "Hospes," the Latin word for hospice, means both host and guest. This meaning puts the emphasis on the process of caring and learning. It is an interaction among human beings which is perceived as simple and mutual. If life is considered a journey, then dying people have more information and knowledge to share about the journey since they have traveled further than any of us. We, in turn, can offer refreshment and attend to physical, emotional and spiritual needs that they are too tired or weak to attend to on their own. The host-guest concept is a fitting explanation of hospice.

The first hospice patient assigned to me was Sam, someone I had known for years. Sam was admitted to Hospice of Louisville on June 13, 1989 with advanced prostate cancer and given little time to live.

Sam and I first met in 1972 at St. Augustine, an all black inner city parish. Before working for Hospice & Palliative Care of Louisville, I was a Roman Catholic priest for 15 years. Sam attended both my deaconate ordination in 1973 and my priesthood ordination in 1974. I wondered how Sam and his wife Jean might react to my life change.

When I first visited Sam's family on August 29, 1989, they were thrilled to see a familiar face. Any thoughts of non-acceptance vanished. They welcomed me with open arms, immediately calling me "Bob" instead of "Father Bob". We both witnessed the ministry of hospice care.

I visited Sam and his wife, Jean, on a weekly basis for two years. During that time he was confined to bed or wheelchair. His legs became paralyzed as his illness progressed. Nurses managed Sam's pain; social workers helped with other needs. One expressive art therapist met with Sam's grandson, TyJuan, to help him deal with Sam's illness.

As a hospice chaplain, my role was to give spiritual and emotional support. They were an ecumenical family with both Catholic and Baptist roots. To conclude every visit we gathered around Sam's hospital bed and formed a prayer circle. We prayed for healing, acceptance and inner peace.

Every weekly visit was unique. On October 8th Sam felt depressed, sad and tearful. The following week he was eating sardines, laughing and joking. The next week he felt guilty for being sick, for being a pain and burden to his family, and for not being able to worship in church.

Sam knew he was deeply loved. His family showed constant love for him and for one another. They did so through a family tradition of greeting one another with three short, gentle, consecutive kisses. Sometimes Sam was overwhelmed by the love of family and friends. This was evident as his home was wallpapered with greeting cards. Jean orchestrated an enormous seventieth birthday party for Sam in July of 1990. Sam rose to the occasion and stayed up for the entire party, not missing anything.

Sam died on March 3, 1992. Since then, Jean developed a serious illness and also benefited from hospice care. Again, I had the privilege to serve as hospice chaplain.

Dr. Cicely Saunders, the founder of modern day hospice care said, "You matter because you are you. You matter to the last moment of your life, and we will do all we can not only to help you die peacefully, but also to live until you die." Our motto for all hospice patients is that they live all the days of their lives.

Lessons From the Tombstones

I find myself writing this down because I don't ever want to forget the way it was. The tombstones told me that things change.

The names on the stones all greeted me that first day, Fred Bauer, Sr., 1964; Marie Newman & Son, 1942; Edward L. Gutgsell, 1967. Pillars of gray stone and weather-beaten limbs met the overcast horizon. A bearded young man flexed to drive a peg into the earth while an elderly gentleman flung heaps of grass along a steady path. Announcing "head first" to an undertaker and six pall bearers, a figure draped in a dilapidated gray coat proceeded up the hillside. This was Calvary Cemetery in Louisville and the description fits today as it did more than 35 years ago.

People look askance when you inform them you are a cemetery worker and even more bewildered when you retort, "People are dying to get in." In the summer of 1966 I felt rather bizarre at the cemetery, constantly in fear of treading over the deceased, and frequently referred to myself as a "cemetarian" rather than as a seminarian (my major role). Yet I had given little thought to the mystery and sting of death until those five summers I worked at Calvary Cemetery.

A lot can happen in five summers. Things change. New personalities, modern funeral equipment, and a larger cemetery accompanied my own personal growth from age 18-22. Some things never change. These are time, silence, peace and death. All are living realities and probably no novel or academic dissertation can spell out life's meaning better than a gingko tree swaying in the wind or a stationary stone bearing a person's name.

One element I found most noteworthy was people's reaction to death. Normally I witnessed widows bawling and moaning "Oh No!" with tears from even the huskiest of males. Sometimes there were emotionless funerals with apathy reigning. Yet Americans must rival their neighbors even to the grave, vying for more extravagant monuments and more expensive plots. Often people visiting Calvary seemed to dwell in the past and living only for their own impending deaths. So many fail to live every moment to the fullest and to celebrate life as it was intended.

Many times I remember a popular visitor who often passed through the black and gold cemetery gates, sauntering down the cobblestone road with a ragged newspaper sack slung over his right shoulder. It's "Skippy," a 75 year old gent, gathering mushrooms and enjoying his afternoon stroll through the cemetery. Skippy hailed from a small German village, leaving his home country with his parents as a child. He had spent his adult life working as a printing press operator. With a beautiful German accent he constantly spoke of his "Fatherland" while commenting on the peace and serenity he found in the cemetery. Skippy (as his nickname relates) was filled with a zest for living which included sauerkraut, beer, picking mushrooms and chatting with cemetery workers. He had experienced death many times and often ambled through section after section informing us of different friends there. He accepted death. Skippy, in suspenders and faded flannel shirt, lived the answer to life.

Calvary Cemetery provides a great deal of spiritual thought and inspiration. I am always impressed by the number of people in these hallowed grounds - people who have eaten, drunk, prayed and struggled through life - people who sinned and cheated their way to the pinnacle of affluence, success and fame. Here they all lie together in peaceful slumber.

Even though I was in my early twenties, I realized how quickly the years of my life were passing by. Looking back, the days of my childhood seem like yesterday. How clear and sharp the memories of those I have loved and lost, bringing a lump to my throat, a tear to my eye. I remember those lives were deeply entwined with mine and from whom I am now parted by death. I have come face to face with the stark truth that, in spite of my yearning for life, I too must one day die. In all I do, thanks to my lessons at Calvary Cemetery, that perspective makes a big difference. Like Skippy, I have found the answer to truly living my life.

PART TWO
OUR QUEST FOR PEACE

Green Pastures

One morning as I was hurriedly dressing to begin a full day, I felt a sharp pain in my back. I mentioned it to my wife, but I was sure it would soon pass. Months of agony followed as the pain persisted. Concerned by the lingering pain my spouse insisted I see a physician who immediately admitted me to the hospital.

I was not happy. I didn't have time to waste there in bed. My calendar was full of activities and commitments, which my doctor insisted I cancel and plan on at least a month for recuperation. A dear minister friend came to visit me during that time. He sat down and in a very firm voice said, "Bob, I have only one thing to say to you – He makes me lie down."

I lay there thinking about those words in the Twenty-Third Psalm long after my friend had left. I thought about how the shepherd starts the sheep grazing about 4 a.m. The sheep walk steadily as they graze; they are never still. By 10 a.m. the sun beams down and the sheep are hot, tired and thirsty. The wise shepherd knows the sheep must neither drink when they are hot, nor when their stomachs are filled with undigested grass. So the shepherd makes the sheep lie down in green pastures, in a cool, soft spot. The sheep will not eat lying down, so they chew their cuds, which is their way of digesting food.

Study the lives of great people, and you will find every one of them drew apart from the hurry of life for rest and reflection. Great poems are not written in the midst of clamoring multitudes; our creative visions from God come when we stop. Sometimes God puts us on our backs in order to give us a chance to look up, "He makes us lie down." Many times we are forced, not by God, but by circumstances of one sort or another to lie down. That always can be a blessed experience. Even the bed of an invalid may be a blessing if he or she takes advantage of it! As Whittier says,

"Take from our souls the strain and stress,
And let our ordered lives confess –
The beauty of Thy peace."

Also, we need to recreate our souls. A group of American explorers went to Africa. They employed some native guides. On the first day they rushed forward, as they did also on the second, third, and on the subsequent days. On the seventh day they noticed the guides sitting under a tree. "Come on," the explorers shouted. One of the guides answered, "We will not go today. We rest today to let our souls catch up with our bodies."

An old miner once explained to a visitor, "I let my mules spend one day a week outside the mines to keep them from going blind." People who never spend time away from the daily grind of life go blind in their souls. The philosopher Santayana tells us, "A fanatic is one who, having lost sight of his aim, redoubles his effort." Much of the feverish haste we see today is by aimless, purposeless people.

We have a slang expression, "That got my goat." The phrase has an interesting source. Owners of sensitive, high-strung race horses kept a goat in the stalls with the horses. The very presence of the calm, relaxed goat helped the horses to relax. On the day before an important race rival owners would sometimes steal another owner's goats in hopes it would cause the goat-less horses to not run their best race the next day.

We all get sensitive and high strung occasionally, and so we falter in the race of life. We need relaxed recreation and spiritual inspiration to be refreshed. We must lie down in green pastures.

Security Can Be Yours

One of the greatest desires of the human heart is to feel secure. Some psychologists say that our desire for security is an instinct. Certainly we all want security though many of us do not have it.

The following are some steps that will help gain security:

1. **Train yourself to be happy with what you can afford.** I know some very miserable people who are struggling to maintain a standard of living far beyond their means. It's a terrible way to exist.

2. **No matter how little you earn, save a little.** I don't sell insurance but I could because I believe in it strongly. A few dollars invested or put in a savings account will bring far more satisfaction than some gadget we strain to buy.

3. **Never lose the spirit of adventure.** Be willing to dream and to dare. Columbus would never have discovered a new world had he always been afraid to get out of sight of land. In life there is something greater than merely taking care of one's self. Be willing to risk a little.

4. **Get acquainted with as many people as you can.** There can be strong security in your friendships. Also, when you come to know the problems of other people and see how they have overcome them, you will gain more confidence.

5. **Realize that there is always a way out if you do your best.** Even your troubles may prove to be your greatest blessings.

A man once put a sparrow egg in a canary's nest. The mother canary hatched the egg and mothered the little sparrow from the day of its birth. Day by day the baby sparrow heard the singing of the canary, and by the time it was grown it could sing like a canary. The man said it was very difficult to tell the difference between the singing of the sparrow and the singing of the canary. If a common sparrow can learn to sing like a canary, then it is reasonable to believe that any of us can learn almost anything into which we put our mind and effort. We can learn to have an inside calm, cooling contentment, no matter what the conditions may be outside.

A simple way to start this learning process is to practice for just one week, concentrating on maintaining an inner calm. You will quickly begin to feel a distinct difference. When you awaken in the morning and before you get out of bed, tell yourself that it is going to be a great day. As you sit down to breakfast, look at your family and tell yourself how lucky you are to have them. When you get to your workplace, instead of complaining about the crowded bus or the heavy traffic, think of how wonderful it is that so many other people have a job and are going to work.

This may sound a bit silly, but keep it up all day. Look for something good in every situation and concentrate on that. Keep that up for just one week and the next weekend will be one of your happiest. When we feel that our lives are in harmony with the will of God, then no matter what our lot in life may be, we have joy in living it.

"Be of good cheer, my brother, for I feel the bottom and it is sound." Those are the words of Hopeful in *Pilgrim's Progress*. You remember how, in his journey to the city of God, the pilgrims came to the last dark river. Hopeful, as hope always does, led the way and in the very midst of the river called back that assuring word.

As we look back over the journey of life, we see many trials and hardships, but for many there is still a dark river ahead. Now there are two ways of looking at the future. One is to concentrate on the dark river. The other is to say, "Be of good cheer my brother, for I feel the bottom and it is sound." We must think of the sound bottom instead of the river.

A man who was thinking of taking his life came to see me. He told me he had lost everything and therefore had no reason to live. I asked what he had lost and he said it was his business and every dollar he had. I used a technique with him I learned from Dr. Norman Vincent Peale.

I took a sheet of paper and drew a line down the center. On one side I wrote "losses" and on the other side wrote "assets." In the losses column I wrote "business and money." I asked if he had lost anything else. He said, "That's all, but that is everything." "Has your wife left you?" I asked. "Oh no," he said, "she still loves me and has taken a job in a department store to help us out." So in the assets column I wrote "wife". I asked about his children. He has two and he assured me they were still loyal to him. So I listed "children" as an asset. "Is there as much opportunity in America today as there was 25 years ago?" was my next question. He assured me there was much more opportunity today. So we wrote down "opportunity" as an asset. His health was good, so that too entered the asset column. Finally, I asked if he believed in God. He did. "God" was added to the asset list.

Then I told him about Hopeful in Pilgrim's Progress and pointed out how he too had come to a dark river. It isn't easy to lose a business you have worked twenty-five years to build, but instead of concentrating on his losses, we talked about focusing on his assets. After all, a man with a loyal wife, children, experience, opportunity, health and God should be able to say sincerely, "Be of good cheer, my brother, the bottom is sound." He left me, realizing that he did have a firm foundation on which to start building again. He realized he had a lot of security in his assets. I believe he went with "good cheer" in his heart.

Mental Peace

All of us have had a childlike peace at one time. But as we grow older, our lives become more complicated. We think of making a living and we worry about our debts, our jobs, or taking care of ourselves in our old age. We bother about the world situation. We get crossed up with other people, we become upset thinking of our health and we want to improve our social position.

We do things that are wrong and we fail to do things that are right, and our consciences hurt. We develop little civil wars inside ourselves. We cannot relax, so we get tense and nervous. Because we do not have peace of mind and peace of soul, we get sick and life becomes an unhappy burden.

A physician friend told me that in many of his cases his treatment was ineffective because the patients were so agitated and upset. He said that before their bodies could be healed, they needed to find mental peace.

If we could only find the childlike perfect peace we had when our bodies were young, life would take on new joys and thrills that many have even forgotten exist. So I want to point out three steps that will help anyone to find mental peace.

1. **Get the poisons out of your mind**. Imagine if you had a pain in your side and you went to the doctor and found that your appendix was badly inflamed and that before you could be well it would have to be taken out. Or maybe it was an abscessed tooth that your dentist discovered that was poisoning your system. The abscess had to be healed before you could regain your health.

More often it is not a physical poison that is hurting you. Is there something on your conscience? Have you done some wrong? Are you angry with anybody? The step to take is to get the poison out of your mind and to forgive yourself and others.

2. **Fill your mind with the right things.** Count
   your many blessings and name them one by one.
   Instead of concentrating on your problems, just sit
   down quietly and identify each of your blessings. It
   may seem a simple thing to do but the results will
   amaze you.

Think of something beautiful. For example, picture two
dozen deep red roses scattered out on a table. Then, in your
imagination, begin to pick them up one by one and arrange
them in a vase. It will take some practice but is surely well
worth the effort. Our imaginations need to be used and
stretched often. Something beautiful in your mind will invite
peace.

3. **Accept your responsibilities and obligations.**
   As we start doing the things we know we should do, it
   makes us feel good inside.

Silas Marner was a bitter, unhappy miser until he lost his
gold and found a little golden haired girl. As he began to love
and live for her, he found happiness and peace. You will
never find peace so long as you think only of your own
interests.

Dante said it best, " In his will is our peace." When our
lives are in harmony with God, we have an instinctive sense of
the right direction, and we move forward with courage and
confidence without fear of getting lost.

Inner Peace

The most important possession of all is inner peace. Even if one has health, love, beauty, talent, power, riches and fame, life can be a hideous torment and an intolerable burden without inner peace.

There are four main reasons why so many people do not know the blessing of inner peace.

1. **We worry about the things we do not have and become dissatisfied with the things we have.**

I once knew an elderly man with whom I spent a lot of time and from whom I learned a lot. He was a wise philosopher. He would tell me of life as it used to be, how very little people had yet how happy they were. One day the mail man left a mail order catalog at one of the neighborhood homes. The family began to look at it, first wonderingly and then longingly.

Soon every house in the community had one of the catalogs. The old man shook his head sadly as he described how the people forgot the beauty of the mountains around them and turned away from the things that used to mean so much. As they turned the pages of the catalogs they could only yearn for the many things they did not possess.

2. **We develop a crisis psychology.** Some crisis is always coming along, such as an unexpected expense, an illness, or one of a thousand other things. Before we realize it, life has become a constant crisis. We must learn not to make a crisis out of every uncomfortable situation in our lives.

3. **Our inner conflicts destroy our inner peace.** We are made with both a higher and lower nature with a constant struggle between the two. Unfortunately some poor souls just give up to the conflict and sink to their lowest level.

The Gentle Art of Caring

4. **There are conflicts between ourselves and other people that destroy our peace.** Our feelings are hurt. We carry a grudge. We have an unforgiving spirit.

What is the best way to visualize restlessness? I think of a rough sea. I have stood on the seashore and watched the continuous movement of the water. I have yet to see it still even for one moment. The water tosses itself upon the shore and then runs back again. Why can't the sea be still? Because it is the victim of a divided mind. The voices of the sky are calling to it. It is drawn up by the magnets of the heavens. But an even stronger pull from the earth demands, "Stay with me." The sea can never completely decide. It is always tossing. It never finds rest or peace.

There are two forces within each person struggling to become the master. One force is ideals, the call of the higher life, the desire to be good and godly. The other force is selfish desires, the worldly nature. Goethe said that it is regrettable that nature made only one man of him when there is plenty of material for both a rogue and a gentleman. We may choose following our own way, but even then we will not have peace because our higher power will never leave us alone. It is as Augustine said, "Man is restless until he finds his rest in Thee, O God."

The Gentle Art of Caring

PART THREE – INTIMACY IN OUR RELATIONSHIPS

Our Need For Close Friendships

Kathy and Anne have played golf every Wednesday for more than ten years. They are very different types of women. Kathy owns a small business and Anne is a commercial artist. But their afternoon on the links is an important ritual that neither violates unless they are out of town.

"We say that we do it for the exercise and the chance to be outdoors," says Kathy, "but the real reason we get together, and we both know it, is to talk. We need to log in with each other at least once a week."

Last year Anne lost her job and was unemployed for almost six months. She says that the Wednesday afternoon talks were one of the things that pulled her through.

All of us are people who need people. As Samuel Johnson says, "If a man does not make new acquaintances as he advances through life, he will soon find himself alone; one should keep his friendships in constant repair."

Yet one of the most illuminating indicators of the human condition, of our predicament and light and fractured status, is that many of us find it so hard to discover what love really does. It couldn't be stranger if fish were afraid of the water and eagles were frightened by the open sky.

And so we understand all too well the literary character Dmitri Karamazov when he says that he would gladly die for the human race, but feels like strangling the man next to him who keeps sniffling. We know what Charlie Brown is going through when he confesses that he loves humanity but can't stand people.

The fact that most of our pressure problems and emotional problems are people problems is one reason why a psychiatrist is different from a book about psychiatry. A psychiatrist is a person, and when you are relating and reacting to a person, things start to happen. Memories stir, fears and needs are triggered, underground testing goes on, tender and hostile feelings surface, masks and disguises go into operation, and subtle transfers of energy take place.

If people are our problem, they are also the solution to our problem. We are either moving toward people, away from people or against people. There will be problems and pressures connected with each of these situations. But as C. M. Schwab says, "Lead the life that will make you kindly and friendly to everyone about you, and you will be surprised what a happy life you will live."

Think of those persons in your life who have approached you from the start as though they were already your friends. I bet you were inclined to respond in a friendly way. By acting as though you were already a friend, they made you friendly. This situation is similar to the way that grownups talk to a child as though the child can understand, and by this procedure they actually bring the child to understand.

There is a beautiful remark in the Jewish Talmud which is applicable: "He who cares for his own child is like a stream which nourishes a tree along its banks. But he who loves another's child is like a cloud which goes from the sea into the desert and waters there a lone and lonesome tree." At a time when American society is being fragmented into so many hostile "in groups" and "out groups", there is no more urgent and timely task than to help break open closed circles.

The proud owner of the world's largest collection of termites, 230,000 of them, says that these insects have a "secret formula" that helps them survive. The formula is that they cooperate with one another. Zoologist Alfred Emerson says that "one of the main ways that termites survive is through cooperation, not competition."

There can be no relationship without conversation. To know and love a friend over the years, you must have regular talks. This may seem perfectly obvious, but I see many close relationships break down because people quit talking. An important guideline for cultivating intimacy is to schedule leisurely breaks for conversation. That's what Kathy and Anne do on the links. That's what we all must do with those who are our dearest friends.

Cultivate Yourself

Through the years I have remembered a story about a girl asking her mother, "Mom, what is personality?" Her reply, "I don't know what it is, but whatever it is, you ain't got it."

The mother was wrong; everyone has personality. The impression you make on other people is really your personality. We wish to achieve to our happiest and best position in life. We need to constantly cultivate our personalities.

First we need to develop a wholesome sense of self-appreciation. One of the most contemptible persons we ever meet is the conceited person. Not many persons are truly conceited, but a lot of people who give that impression really feel inferior in their hearts. No person should ever feel inferior, and one of our greatest mistakes is to underestimate ourselves. We are more than we think we are. We need to pray the prayer that says, "O Lord, give me a higher opinion of myself." Once Abraham Lincoln's mother said to him, "Abe – be somebody." Somehow Abraham Lincoln believed that could be accomplished, and he became about the most important "somebody" who ever lived in our land.

I wish I had the power to plant firmly and securely in the mind of every person to whom I have ever ministered the thought, "You are somebody, and above all, be that somebody."

One of the greatest thinkers and philosophers of all time was Immanuel Kant. Any student of philosophy knows that he was a man whose mind dealt with great thoughts. He summed up his philosophy of life in one sentence: "Two things fill me with ever increasing admiration and awe the longer and more earnestly I reflect upon them; the starry heavens without and the moral law within."

Believing the above to be true, we may begin to seriously release those winsome, lovable personalities within us. We need not wait until we have all the money and all the material things we have dreamed of and want. Houses and cars and clothes and jewelry and savings accounts are all good, but some of the most winsome personalities do not have any of those things.

Even though we did not get all the education we wanted, have not read all the books, and do not know as much as we would like to know, still we can operate with what we have learned and what we do know. Most of us know a lot more than we realize.

Although we may not hold the "dream" position in life, someone is way up the ladder ahead of us and sees that person we become when we are dissatisfied and belittle ourselves. But it is just possible that person is really not as well off as we are. Personality is not dependent upon position.

Your relationships with other people may not be perfect and may even be strained. This can happen between neighbors, between people you work with, between members of your own family.

One night two friends who had not seen each other in many years happened to meet downtown. They walked over to a little restaurant and began talking with each other, reminiscing about their lives. Before they realized it, it was 3 a.m. Both knew their wives would be upset about their staying out so late. However, they went on home. A few days later they met again. One said to the other, "How did you make out getting home so late the other night?" The man replied, "Fine. I just told my wife that I had met you and how we talked together, and she said she understood and that was fine." Then he said, "How did you make out?" The other man replied, "Well, when I came in at 3 a.m., my wife got historical." His friend corrected him saying, "You mean she got hysterical." "No," the man insisted, "I mean historical – she brought up everything that had happened in the last thirty years."

Telling that stupid story reminds me of another one. On their 25th wedding anniversary, the husband said to the wife,

"Honey, I have never deceived you, have I?" "No," she replied, "but you have tried many times."

What I am trying to say here is, there come times when we need to forget past mistakes and past failures and say, "I am who I am and what I am, and I am going to let my personality be the very best it can be." There is no need to wait until all the conditions get perfectly right.

I knew a man who decided he would begin reading some good books. In order to do that he made careful preparations. He selected the comfortable chair in the house and placed it in the room where he planned to read. He put on his slippers and his lounging robe; he fastened a book rest to the arm of the chair to hold the book at just the right angle before his eyes. He set a special reading lamp by his side. After everything was perfectly adjusted, he sat down in his chair and promptly went to sleep.

Many times we spend all our energies in getting everything ready to start, and then we have nothing left with which to start. Most great things are not done in perfect conditions. O'Henry wrote most of his best books while he was in jail. Likewise Saint Paul wrote many of his greatest letters in jail; "Pilgrim's Progress" and "Don Quixote" were written in jail; Sir Walter Scott wrote his "History of the World" in jail. Most of us feel bound in some way, and if we wait until we get out of jail and are perfectly free, we never will do what we can do. You do not become a great personality by trying to get all the outside conditions perfectly right. You become great by rising above the conditions.

In Greek mythology there is a story of how the sirens used to sing and the ships would be lured over onto the rocks and the sailors destroyed. One sea captain worked out a defense. He stuffed the ears of his sailors with wax so they could not hear. However, that not only kept them from not hearing the bad, it also shut them out from hearing the good.

Jason worked out a far better defense. When he prepared to make his voyage, he did not stuff his sailors' ears with wax;

instead he hired the finest singer in the land. His name was Orpheus. When the ships neared the place where the sirens sang, Orpheus would strike his harp and begin to lift a song into the air. The music of Orpheus would be so much more wonderful than the songs of the sirens, the sailors were never tempted to leave their course.

Today many voices call people to ruin and destruction. We never win by trying to merely stop those voices or by stuffing our ears in the voice of life; we need to hear the highest and the best. We need to fill our minds with positive thoughts and our lives with constructive action. We need to cultivate ourselves.

Cultivating Intimacy

Love is that grand emotion that makes your life feel full. The reason love works is that it takes your attention off of you and focuses it on someone more important. To love is to wish the other's highest good.

Blessed are those who cultivate intimacy which is at the heart of love. I believe that there are five ways to cultivate intimacy. I have watched many loving relationships blossom in these ways.

1. **Altruism.** This means that I care about you and not just about myself. The best way to compliment each other is frequently.

A man once told me about a habit that many would say was rather peculiar. For years he had a special date with his wife every Thursday night. He would come home in the afternoon, shave and shower, put on his best suit, and go out and get in his car and leave. In a little while, he would come back and ring the front doorbell. His wife would greet him at the door, and they would sit for a while in the living room and talk. Then they would go out to dinner and a show together. They would drive up to the front door, he would escort her to the door, kiss her goodnight, and then go drive his car into the garage and come in through the back door.

It sounds sort of silly for a man to do that with his wife, but when that man died, his wife watered his grave with tears. Falling in love is easy, but staying in love has to be worked at.

2. **Hospitality.** I welcome you into my life with your uniqueness. I love the quote, "A friend is someone who can see through you and still enjoys the show."

   The following verse about the hospitality of love also captures it well:

   " Love has a hem to its garment
      That touches the very dust;
      It can reach the stains of the street and lanes,
      And because it can, it must." - Anonymous

3. **Service.** I will seek to meet your basic needs. I will accept your quirks, your forgetfulness, and moods.
   Allow each other to be human. "How can I hold the love of my husband or wife?" Learn 400 ways of saying, "I think you are wonderful." The longer you know someone, the easier it is to see faults and want to correct them. Keep expressing appreciation.
4. **Humor.** I will laugh at the futility to be perfect.
   Laughter gives balance. Look for the humor and fun in life. So many get bored because there is no humor. Like John Goodman said so well, "Humor is a wonderful way to prevent a hardening of the attitudes!"
5. **Patience.** I will allow us to proceed at a gradual rate of growth. Two illustrations show the advantage of patience. John Wesley's father once asked his wife, "How could you have the patience to tell that blockhead the same thing 20 times over?" "Why," she replied, "If I had told him but 19 times, I should have lost all my labor.

When Leonardo da Vinci was painting his *Last Supper*, he was chided for standing hours before the canvas without making a stroke. He explained: "When I pause the longest, I make the most telling strokes with my brush."

The Gentle Art of Caring

PART FOUR–ACTIONS FOR RESULTS AND HAPPINESS

Right or Wrong

"What's right and what's wrong?" This is a question all of us struggle with and one which few of us agree on the answer.

Many years ago a great preacher declared, "Behind a great deal of our modern immorality is not so much downright badness as a sincere confusion as to what is right and what is wrong."

There are those who would say, "Let your conscience be your guide," or "If it feels good, do it." It's usually good to listen to your conscience and your inner feelings, yet a cannibal can kill and eat you with a perfectly clear conscience. A conscience must be trained within the society's guidelines.

Traveling along life's pathway, we come to those places where we are sincerely confused, and we may suffer the remainder of our days if we make a mistake.

Allow me to suggest four simple guides that will help us decide in the midst of confusion, what is right and what is wrong.

1. **Would you need to keep it a secret?** Things we need to hide are usually wrong. When there are questions to be feared, eyes to be avoided or subjects which must not be broached, my guess is that it is wrong.

2. **Where will it lead me?** Many seemingly harmless little things are wrong because they lead in the wrong direction. A friend of mine loves playing checkers. He used to study the "book moves" and played with the experts. He told me, "At the start of a game of checkers you are free to move in any direction, but once you have moved, your turn is over. Each move

should be carefully considered to positively affect future moves."

Life is pretty much like that. Every action affects future actions. A little lie must be covered by a bigger lie. We can start on a wrong path in a harmless way, gradually getting too far down to win the game.

3. Which is your best self? We all have more than one "self." There is our passionate self. We sometimes say and do things when we are angry or afraid or under the power of lust.

Then there is our careless self. We just drift along, not taking the time or making the effort to really think. There is the greedy self, when we are thinking only of our interest and disregarding the rights and interests of others. How many times have you heard someone say, "I just wasn't myself." It's wise to be very careful when we are not "ourselves."

Within each of us there is a "best self," which is so much finer than the passionate or careless or greedy self. Shakespeare urges us, "To thine own self be true, and it must follow as the night the day, thou canst not then be false to any man."

4. What would the person whom you most admire do if they were in your place? It's not always easy to decide what is right and what is wrong.

If we sincerely want to do the right thing, these four simple guides will be a lot of help along the way.

Get a Cause Today

How do I go about finding a purpose in life? How do I discover my cause?

One of the first answers to that would be, "What do I like most to do?" Really, that involves my desires, my abilities, and my opportunities. I do not like the expressions "sacred" and "secular" in reference to work. To me all work is sacred. Being a good mechanic is just as sacred as is being a good minister. We need to use our talents, not bury them. The very using of our talents carries with it the possibilities of defeat. Defeat is certainly a badge of greatness. Nobody wants to lose, but on the other hand, it is a lot worse to bury ourselves without taking chances or doing anything. Defeat is not easy to bear but not to have the nerve to take the chance that living requires is a lot worse.

There is a legend that once a king placed a heavy stone in the middle of the road. The people who came down that road grumbled about having to walk around that stone. Finally, one man came along, saw the obstacle, and set about the job of moving it. Under the stone he found a purse of gold. So it is in life. Take the chance. For your efforts you may taste disappointment, but you may find gold. It takes faith to commit your life to something, not knowing how it will turn out. Those who are willing to risk, however, are the people who gain the victories. Remember, every defeat also is a possible victory.

In my own counseling with many unhappy people who feel defeated and who have given up on life (and given up on themselves), I have suggested they take a sheet of paper and begin writing down some of the reasons for living. We give up and quit because we decide there is no reason for living. Finding a reason for living immediately gives one a new power. The best nerve medicine on this earth is a life purpose.

George Bernard Shaw suggested that an appropriate epitaph for a lot of people would be "died at thirty, buried at sixty." In contrast, I like the spirit of the old man who said, "I am going to live until I die, and then I am going to live forever." A lot of people worry about the wrong thing. They worry about life after death when they ought to be worrying about life after birth. If a person is properly concerned about living, then that individual is not improperly worried about eternity.

Never miss an opportunity to express appreciation for something. Really, what life is all about is our relationships – people loving and helping each other – we get and we give – we are thankful. Then we find it easier to accept life, and as we accept life, we find peace.

Here are some words that inspire me:

"Celebrate the temporary –
Don't wait until tomorrow
Live today.
Celebrate the simple things –
Enjoy the butterfly
Embrace the snow
Run with the ocean
Delight in the trees
Or a single lonely flower
Go barefoot
In the wet grass.
Don't wait
Until all the problems
Are solved
Or all the bills
Are paid.
You will wait forever
Eternity will come and go
And you
Will still be waiting.
Live in the now

With all its problems
      And its agonies
With its joy
      And its pain
Celebrate your pain –
      Your despair
         Your anger
It means you're alive
      Look closer
      Breathe deeper
      Stand taller
Stop grieving the past.
There is joy and beauty
      Today
It is temporary
      Here now and gone
So celebrate it
      While you can
Celebrate the temporary."
         -Anonymous

Give Out Positive Energy

One night, when Robert Louis Stevenson was six years old, he watched the lamplighter work. One by one, the lighter lit the lamps as he walked down the street. Young Stevenson remained fascinated and silent. His nurse feared that his quietness meant he was up to some mischief. She called out, asking what he was doing. The little child answered, "I am watching a man making holes in the darkness." What a difference the lamplighter made by giving out positive energy.

I love Edith Wharton's quote: "There are two ways of spreading light: to be a candle, or the mirror that reflects it." There's also D. L. Moody's statement: "A holy life will produce the deepest impression. Lighthouses blow no horns; they only shine." There are so many qualities of light to reflect on that inspire us to give our light and energy to others.

1. **One of the qualities of light is that it cannot be soiled.** Your hands may be covered with dirt, but when you grasp a beam of light, you leave no mark of that dirt upon it. You may shine a beam into the worse filth, but none of it will stick to the light. So, one who is the light will not be soiled in any circumstance or situation.

2. **Light is one of the most cheerful and cheering things this world knows.** Admiral Robert E. Peary discovered the North Pole. Telling about the long journey there, he said that the greatest obstacle he overcame in the Artic was not the cold, but the long darkness. The continual absence of light took away the spirit of the men. One of the worst punishments you can inflict upon any person is to cause him to stay in absolute darkness for an extended period of time.

Every physician knows that people can be in pain during the day and bear it, but, as the darkness comes and as the night moves on, the pain becomes unbearable to the point where they can stand it no longer. Physicians understand why many people phone for help at night when they might not phone during the day.

3. **The light also reveals the way; it is a guide.** Someone conducted an experiment with a group of people to test their powers of observation. The people entered a room and stayed for a period of time. Then they left and made a list of the room's content. Nearly every list included items people saw with their eyes. The room contained many other things such as the fragrance of flowers, the sound of music, the warmth from a heater, and the softness of the chairs. But the people were impressed more by what they saw than by what they smelled or heard or felt. Truly sight is our main source of knowledge, and it is because of light that we see.

A lovely flower and an ugly weed really are the same in the dark. It is only when we throw the light upon them that we see their difference. It is only in the light that we see ourselves – our failures and mistakes – and our great possibilities.

4. **Light makes shadows.** In his play <u>Macbeth</u>, Shakespeare wrote this line, "Life's but a walking shadow." Sometimes we are almost overwhelmed by the deep shadows which fall across our world and our lives. We become discouraged as we see the plagues of vice and crime over our world, the horror of war, discrimination against people, the low state of morals, and all the other shadows. But let us remember that shadows are created by light, and if there were no light there would be no shadows. The fact that we see shadows in our world is evidence of the existence of light, and thus the shadows become a source of encouragement

and strength. The brighter the light, the deeper the shadows.

5. **Another thing about light is that, in order to be light, it must be consumed.** A candle cannot give light without, at the same time, giving itself. Thus, to be a light is a very costly process.

6. **Finally, each individual light is important.** We need to see. We speak often of hypocrites, and certainly we do not mean it as a complimentary term. Normally, we think of hypocrites as people who appear to be better than they really are. But there is another side to the coin: hypocrites are those who fail to appear as good as they really are. We can be hypocrites by refusing to speak out at the proper time or by not providing good example. A candle loses nothing by lighting another candle.

If all the matches produced in France were laid end to end they would stretch eight times the distance between the earth and the moon, or so the state-controlled match industry reports. What power to dispel darkness one little match has, if used properly. And what power for destruction when used carelessly.

Be an example. As the Chinese proverb so aptly states: "Don't curse the darkness. Light a candle." Give out positive energy.

The Gentle Art of Caring

Hope for the Future

Someone pointed out that we live in two worlds – the world that is and the world we want. Faith takes hold of the world that is and makes it what we want it to be. Faith takes the possible and makes it real. It was the great William James who said, "As the essence of courage is to stake one's life on a possibility, so the essence of faith is to believe that the possibility exists." By believing that a better tomorrow is possible, we have the courage to give our best to tomorrow's creation.

Years ago I watched an 80 year old man plant a small peach tree in his yard. I asked him, "You don't expect to eat peaches from that tree, do you?" The old man rested on his spade. He said, "No, at my age, I know I won't. But all my life I have enjoyed peaches, but never from a tree I planted myself. I'm just trying to pay back the other fellows who planted the trees for me to enjoy." **It is so important for us to give back.**

I love the story about a rich man who wanted to do good. One day he noticed the miserable conditions in which a poor carpenter lived. The rich man called the carpenter in and commissioned him to build a beautiful house. "I want this to be an ideal cottage. Use only the best materials, employ only the best workers, and spare no expense." He said that he was going on a journey and that he hoped the house would be finished when he returned.

The carpenter saw this as a great opportunity. He skimped on materials, hired inferior workers at low wages, covered their mistakes with paint and cut corners wherever he could. When the rich man returned, the carpenter brought him the key and said, "I have followed your instructions and built your house as you told me to." "I'm glad," said the rich man; and, handing the keys back to the builder, he continued, "Here are the keys. They are yours. I had you build this house for yourself. You and your family are to have it as my gift."

In the years that followed, the carpenter never ceased to regret the way in which he cheated himself. "Had I only known," he would say to himself, "that I was building this house for myself..." **We must give every effort our very best.**

The ability to think of the future is one of our greatest blessings. If wisely used, this ability causes us to plan and work for tomorrow. The realization that tomorrow will come is the basis of all hope. We are the only creatures on earth who can hope, because only we have the ability to think of tomorrow.

Over the triple doorway of the Cathedral of Milan, there are three inscriptions spanning the splendid arches. Over one is carved a beautiful wreath of roses, and underneath is the legend: "All that pleases is but for a moment." Over the arch on the other side is sculptured a cross, and these are the words beneath: "All that troubles is but for a moment." But underneath the main aisle's great central entrance is the inscription: "That only is important which is eternal."

The Mile That Gets You There

I love the expression I've heard from my Dad and in many sermons and inspirational books: "Don't stop with one mile, go a second mile."

The phrase goes back to Roman times. There was a most annoying law which allowed a Roman soldier to compel any non-Roman citizen to carry his pack for a mile. A man might be hurrying on some important mission for himself when a soldier would see him and demand, "Pick up this pack of mine and carry it a mile." He didn't ask; he commanded. The non-Romans walked that one mile, cursing under their breaths. Since under the law one mile was the limit a soldier could command from a person at any one time, we can feel certain they carefully counted their steps and did not go one step farther than the law demanded.

"Don't stop with one mile, go a second mile." The first mile was compulsory; the second mile was voluntary. The first mile one must go; the second mile one chooses to go. Living really begins after one walks the mile of duty and then steps out on the mile of privilege.

The second mile eliminates life's drudgery. In one of his books William James talks about our "first layer of fatigue." We push and work to the point of exhaustion. We say, "I am so tired, I could drop." James says that most people operate within the limitation of this first fatigue. They never really accomplish much. But he explains that beyond this first fatigue there is almost inexhaustible power. He says, "The people who do great things are those who drive past this first fatigue."

Runners on a track team speak of catching their "second wind." After they run for a time, runners' legs get heavy and they begin to slow down. But runners keep going and suddenly they gain new strength. Their legs are no longer tired and they begin to breathe easier; they pick up speed.

Just as airplanes can break through the "sound barrier," so can people break through the "fatigue barrier." The point where one breaks through this barrier is that place where we begin "the second mile."

Many people go through life doing only those things they are compelled to do. They find life hard, without much joy, and they are constantly tired. Other people go beyond the call of duty and freely give of themselves on a voluntary basis. They find life stimulating and thrilling.

The first mile is compulsion. The second mile is consecration. On the first mile people are constantly demanding their "rights". On the second mile they constantly look for their opportunities. The mile of duty is no fun. On the mile of consecration we find great joy.

Once my mother sent me to pick a quart of blackberries. I despised picking blackberries, but she commanded me to do so, and I went to the patch in a rebellious mood. I resented living in a world where little boys had to pick berries when they wanted to play. As I picked the berries, suddenly I had an idea. It would be fun to surprise the family at dinner that night. Instead of one quart of berries, they would have two and everyone could have an extra helping. Thinking about surprising my family, I hurriedly and happily picked the first and then the second quart. I never enjoyed anything more. That is the way the second mile principle works all the way through life. If we go beyond mere duty and compulsion, we find new strength and happiness.

Not only does the second mile eliminate life's drudgery, it also is the mile on which we make our progress. People who think only of their duty never really succeed, when people think in terms of voluntary consecration, they get enthusiastic. We never find enthusiasm in the things we are compelled to do, but we do find enthusiasm in the things we want to do. The word "enthusiasm" is derived from the

Greek words "en Theos," meaning "in God" or "inspired by God."

The second mile rewards us in our relationships with other people. As we go along through life, somebody will do us wrong. There are four attitudes we may take:

1. "If they hurt me, I will hurt them more" – that is vindictiveness.
2. "If they hurt me, I will treat them the same" – that is retribution, the old law of "an eye for an eye."
3. "If they hurt me, I will ignore them and have nothing more to do with them" – that is disdain.
4. "If they hurt me, I will love and serve them" – that is the way that brings rewards.

A man moved into a house next door to a friend of mine. After a few days, the new neighbor phoned my friend angrily to tell him that his driveway was two feet over their property line. He demanded that they employ a surveyor. My friend said, "We do not need a surveyor. You go out and set some stakes where the line should be and I'll move my driveway. I'll accept your judgment in the matter."

He didn't hear any more from the neighbor for several days and neither did he see any stakes. One day they met in the yard and my friend asked about the line. The neighbor said, "Oh, forget the line. There is enough for both of us, and two feet one way or the other makes no difference." My friend went the second mile and in so doing he won the neighbor's friendship.

You Always Have A Move

All of us miss something we would like to have. Every person must face some blockade along the pathway to happiness and success in life. When that blockade impedes your progress, what can you do about it? If you take a positive attitude you can hurdle the handicap that holds you back. You always have a move. But it's hard. It's much easier to surrender to some negative attitude such as rebellion or self-pity.

At some time in life, nearly every person arrives at a place which seems to be the "end of the world." We remember Miss Haversham in Dickens' Great Expectations. With elaborate wedding preparations made, her lover jilted her. In grief and humiliation, Miss Haversham closed all the blinds of the house, stopped every clock, left the wedding cake on the table to gather cobwebs, and continued to wear her wedding dress until it hung in yellow decay about her shrunken form. Her disappointment became her "end of the world."

A great violinist was giving a concert when the "A" string on his violin broke. Without hesitating he transposed the music and finished the concert on three strings. A lesser violinist might have stopped and moaned about his bad luck. It takes a great artist to say, "If I can't play on four strings, I will play on three."

So it is in life. Hardly anyone has all he or she wants. We can complain about our bad fortune, or we can go ahead and produce melody with what we have.

I read about a traveler who fell down the side of a mountain and was knocked unconscious. Finally, he woke up but had no idea how long he had been there. He lost all sense of time and direction. He looked across the valley and saw the sun just above the horizon, but could not tell whether the sun was rising or setting. For the first time he realized that, rising or setting, the sun looks the same.

Experiences come upon us that change our lives. Sometimes our fondest dreams are thwarted. We are very conscious of our weaknesses and limitations. It is so easy to feel that everything is lost, that life from now on will not be worth living. But it may be (it often is) that which we thought was the sun setting is the sunrise. There may be more light ahead than we thought possible. What seemed to be the end may be the new beginning.

People I admire are the teachers at The de Paul School in Louisville's Highlands. The de Paul School is a school for students with dyslexia, those who have difficulty with printed language. The teachers at de Paul see dyslexia as a gift. They see dyslexia less as a learning disability than as a teaching disability. Often the real disability is in those of us who cannot see our own blockades and lack of understanding. Our task is to reach out to others.

There is a painting which shows the devil at a chessboard with a young man. The devil has just made his move and the young man's queen is checkmated. On his face is written defeat and despair. One day a chess genius stood looking at that painting. Carefully he studied the positions on the board. Suddenly his face lit up and he shouted to the young man in the painting. "You still have a move! Don't give up! You still have a move!"

We come to those moments when it seems we are checkmated. We see no winning move we can make. Don't give up. You still have a move. All things are possible!

Steps To Self Confidence

One of the classic poems of all time is Robert Browning's *Rabbi be Ezra* in which he said:
"Grow old along with me!
The best is yet to be,
The last of life, for which the first was made.
Our times are in his hand
Who saith: 'A whole I planned,
Youth shows but half; trust God; see all, nor be afraid!'"
We might think, "With his beloved Elizabeth at his side, of course, Robert Browning could write those words." The truth is when Browning wrote "Grow Old Along With Me," Elizabeth had been dead for three years. The great poet's life was shattered. During those three years he accomplished very little. At that time he was well past the age of 50. He wanted to run away and hide, but he faced up to his own character and felt that he should be more of a man than a coward. He began thinking of one whom he admired for many years, the twentieth-century scholar Rabbi ben Ezra. Among other things Rabbi ben Ezra preached, "Approach the twilight of life with joy and hope. Approach the last of life with eagerness, not gloom. For the last of life is the best of life. Trust God and be not afraid."

Browning was inspired to write a poem on the rabbi's teachings. He gave himself completely over to it. Many of us feel it became his crowning effort. The point is that he was alone when he wrote "Grow Old Along With Me." That should give us assurance and inspiration when we feel our confidence fading.

You can divide life into two major divisions. The years under 50 are the years of physical as well as mental vitality. The years after fifty also are years of mental vitality with greatly increased spiritual vitality.

Look at age 50, which I consider sort of the dividing line. It really is the time of new birth – the time to start new hobbies, develop new interests, even begin new careers. On the other hand, it can start the "shriveling up" era of your life. Diseases can become more prominent. You might begin to think of yourself as weaker and sicker. It can be a time of giving up instead of growing up.

Then comes the time of retirement. We can think of ourselves as "rocking chair" cases or remember that Thomas Edison created the electric light bulb in his mid 60's and use that for incentive. This really is the time for new ideas, the time to re-tire. It is the time to forget about that big rest and begin tuning in on the millions of ideas in this glorious universe.

Beyond 60 we can experience mental and spiritual growth as never before. Out of a ripened intellect can come our greatest ideas, our deepest understandings, and our finest joys. These are the years that prove how you have lived and what you have put in to your life. Never believe that you will just dry up and blow away at age 70. Above all things at this age search out happiness. It is the most wonderful of all life preservers.

> "Age is like a mountain high;
> Rare is the air and blue-
> A long, hard climb and a little fatigue-
> But, oh! What a wonderful view!
> -Author Unknown

Whatever your age, one of the first things you must do is gain self confidence. All of my life I have been a student of Abraham Lincoln. I believe he is the greatest American who ever lived. If you really know Lincoln, you know that his greatest problem was his doubts about himself, doubts that lasted until he died. Self-confidence alluded him, but he fought to get past his doubts and did not allow them to defeat him. There are several steps to real self-confidence, no matter what your age.

1. **Set a major life goal for yourself.** Forget about your achievements or your failures. Begin right now and get yourself a new target. Start saying to yourself and keep saying it until you really believe it, "This which I have decided to do, I can do."

2. **Do not overly worry about making decisions.** Even if you make a mistake, you can correct it.

3. **Talk about your fears to somebody else.** Just the expression of your fears tends to overcome them.

4. **Do not forget to laugh.** Laugh at yourself, laugh with other people and laugh at your world.

5. **Remember that other people have many of the same doubts, worries and problems you have.** Be sympathetic, kind and thoughtful of others. Not only should you think of what you can do for yourself and what you can accomplish, but also perform acts of kindness that will bring strength, courage or relief to others.

6. **Remember that you are never alone.** Even if your loved ones are too busy for you, or if you have only a few friends, there is a Power that we feel and can tap into through frequent prayer and meditation.

Go back to Robert Browning's beautiful poem, "Grow old along with me! The best is yet to be." In each of our lives let's emphasize the line "the best is yet to be." No matter what your station in life, believe that your present age is the best age, and it is very likely to be so.

Give Your Best
to the Present Moment

I like the story of a famous old naturalist who began to cut trees to build a log house. A friend said to him, "Isn't that a big undertaking for a man of your years?"

He replied, "It would be if I thought of chopping the trees, sawing the logs, skinning the bark, laying the foundation, erecting the walls, and putting on the roof. Carrying the load all at once would exhaust me. But it isn't so hard to cut down this one tree, and that is all I have to do now."

One of the difficulties in living today is that we are burdened by yesterday's decisions. Where is there one among us who has not said, "If I had only made a different decision, my life would be better now?" Suppose you married some other person, or entered some other line of work, or settled in some other city? One help at this point is to remind yourself that you do not know the road you did not take. In your imagination you think of that other road as smooth and straight and leading directly to your heart's desire, but you are not. That other road may have been more wearisome and more heartbreaking.

A second help is to remind yourself that you have not seen all of the road which you did choose. Maybe you are having hardships and difficulties now, but who knows – tomorrow may bring a turning point, if not tomorrow, maybe next week, or next month, or next year. It is just possible that the road on which you are now traveling will run head on into happiness, the happiness you thought was on the road you did not choose.

One day, Lloyd George and a friend were walking across a field. As they walked, his friend asked Lloyd George how he had kept his inner composition and strength during the First World War's difficult days. As they came to the end of the field, Mr. George opened the gate, and after they walked through, he carefully closed it. Then he said, "Right here is my secret. I always close the gate behind me and concentrate on where I am walking now." **To give our best to the present, we must close the gates of the past.**

Second, we must realize that many of today's hardships and unhappiness are not permanent. Someone once asked an old retired minister what his favorite Bible passage was. Quickly came his reply: "And it came to pass." He went on to explain that through a long life he had come to realize that the heartaches, troubles, wars, debts, and all the burdens of life "come to pass."

This same truth applies to life's happy, delightful experiences as well. We need to learn to enjoy the joys of each day, because they too "come to pass." Wouldn't it be wonderful if we could keep our precious little children in our homes, just as they are, so that one day, when we had time, we could play with them and enjoy them? But that little child doesn't stay that way. A child has growing power, and if we expect to enjoy our children, we have to enjoy them when we have the opportunity. In reference to both our burdens and our pleasures, let us remember that they do "come to pass." Knowing that truth, we can face them squarely day by day.

Third, in living one day at a time, we must not try to run ahead into tomorrow. Isn't it true that most of our worries are borrowed from tomorrow? We worry about mountains we may never have to climb, about streams we may never have to cross, about enemies we may never have to face. One points out that insurance companies become rich by betting that what people worry about will never happen.

One assurance that helps us overcome our fears for tomorrow is the fact that we will be given the strength we need. Once an infuriated bull chased a boy across a field. The boy leaped over a high fence and saved himself. Sometimes later, the boy went back to that fence and tried to jump again. He tried, but never again jumped over that fence, yet in his moment of great need he possessed unusual strength.

What we do is to anticipate our future needs, and we try to match them with our present resources. We fail to consider our strength and ability repeatedly when those needs arise. You are stronger than you think. You are braver than you think. Wait until the need arises before you begin to worry about it.

Thomas S. Kepler in one of his books tells about a group of 104 psychologists who studied their cases and determined an anxiety timetable: At 18, we worry about ideals; at 20, we worry about appearance; at 23, about morals; at 26 about making a good impression; at 30, about salary and the cost of living; at 31, about business success; at 33, about job security; at 41, about politics; at 42, about marital problems; at 45, about the loss of ambition; over 45, about health. Most of our worries are useless.

As we put our best into the living of each day, we go a long way toward the elimination of our worries, fears, and anxieties.

Your Facial Expression

I went into a photographer's studio to have my picture taken. I went with great reluctance, because I firmly believed in my mind that I would not take a good picture.

"This is something I hate to do," I told the photographer. "I haven't had a picture taken in years. I'm definitely not photogenic."

"I wish you had not said that," answered the photographer. "There is no reason why you shouldn't take a fine picture. However, if you feel like that about it, chances are you will not take a good picture."

"But, I feel this because of previous experiences," I explained.

"You probably had a picture made that wasn't good. When you had the picture taken, doubt came between you and the camera. Consequently, the picture did not turn out good," the photographer reasoned.

"But," I persisted, "How can there be doubt showing in a photograph?"

"I don't know how to explain it, but it is evident in the photograph. What you think shows in the picture. Something almost tangible lies between you and the film," replied the photographer.

I knew that he was right. As I prepared to face the camera, I sang a little tune that I liked. It cheered me up. I had faith that the photographer would get a good picture. I composed myself and put the expression on my face that I wanted to come across on the picture. The photographer took six poses. Not one of the poses could be called a poor likeness of me. I had decided what I wanted to look like, and that's exactly what came out on the picture.

This situation can be compared to life. The way we feel about life shows through in the expression on our face. If we are discouraged or downcast, it shows on our face. If we are enthusiastic and optimistic, it shows on our face.

The following story is about a youngster who enjoyed watching an elderly Scotsman work in the early evening.

As a small lad, the boy would sit in an upstairs window every evening during the twilight hours and watch for the coming of the Scotsman, who, by trade, was a lamplighter. The lamplighter, whose job was to light the public street lamps, would zigzag his way down the street, lighting one lamp after another as he went along. Occasionally, the silent, old lamplighter would look up at the window and wave his hand in cheerful greeting to the young watcher. As the lamplighter passed through the street, the evening shadows were penetrated at intervals by the flicking lights he left burning along the way.

To be a lamplighter, in the days of hand-lit street lamps, was a wonderful occupation. Today, it is heartening to contemplate that all of us can be lamplighters. Wherever we go, we should leave a light behind us: the light of a friendly smile, a hearty laugh, a warm handshake, a word of cheer. How wonderful it would be, if, after our passing, someone contemplated our actions and said, "That person was truly a lamplighter. They left a light along the way."

Have You Found Total Happiness?

Today's greatest problem is that we engage ourselves in an anxious search for total happiness and are unable to find it. We want that complete fulfillment and convince ourselves that we will settle for nothing less.

When I speak with people facing unhappiness, I hear the same things over and over, things like: "I'm so bored with life." "We find our relationship limiting." "Something is missing." There is more to life and I want to find it in a new setting."

"What is missing?" I ask. And they usually respond by saying something like this: "What is missing is total and complete happiness."

We try to fill the void with adult toys – new cars, more expensive cars, or we try to find what's lacking in sex, in playing out of human passions, in love affairs, and in physical relationships with some bodies who eventually become nobodies.

We attempt to find what's missing in new techniques and fads, some from the Far East and some from the American West – meditation and yoga, health foods and liquid diets. We are convinced that there is a solution to our imperfect lives, and we are driven to explore and to search, to experiment and look for more, for something else.

In the end, we discover what we should have realized from the beginning, that the search is futile. In the end we confront ourselves with the fact that we are imperfect beings, imperfect people involved with other imperfect people and working in imperfect careers.

There is a solution, if we are only willing to accept it. It has to do with our coming to terms with ourselves and our lives. It has to do with our making peace with the limitations, the imperfections, and the brokenness of our lives.

The sooner we acknowledge the limitations and imperfections of life and living, fulfillment, and that sense of the wholeness we all desire, the better. Supreme happiness does not lie within some perfect career, some perfect job, or some perfect marriage. Happiness and fulfillment lie within our ability to recognize the imperfections within those things and our willingness to strive for perfection in spite of them, even though we never attain it.

Happiness, according to many philosophers, is a state of being that nobody recognizes while they are happy but can recollect all too clearly when they are unhappy.

There are seven traits of happy people that I have observed:

1. Happy people take life "for gratitude" and not "for granted."
2. Happy people live by affirmations rather than by denunciations.
3. Happy people see good in others.
4. Happy people give wholehearted effort to some undertaking. Loafing on the highway never leads to happiness.
5. Happy people are always eager to give and, also, willing to receive.
6. Happy people know that life is too short to be unhappy. Those who have experienced happiness universally testify that the other problems of life either disappear or else solutions are found.
7. Finally, for happy people the problems of life are changed into challenges and opportunities.

It seems paradoxical, but it is true. You find happiness by forgetting about it. You find happiness by giving yourself to some other search.

The Gentle Art of Caring

PART FIVE – CHANGE CAN BE GOOD

Change, Change, Change

One of the constant problems we face is change. Really, we should not link the two words – "problem" and "change" – together, but we do. For most of us, change is a problem. Sometimes we even link the words, "change" and "decay." There is a tendency to feel that change is bad.

I heard a minister say recently, "Since I have been in the church, there have been a lot of changes, and I have been opposed to all of them." The truth of the matter is, most people oppose most changes. Someone wrote this: "Come weal, come woe, My status is quo."

However, the old worn-out phrase still is true: "We live in a world of change." There are changes in our political system, and we divide politically pretty much on the basis of those in favor of change and those in favor of no change. A list of changes in our society would be utterly endless. We see tremendous transformations in the emergence of a multiracial society. Attitudes of the college campus are not the same as they used to be. In the greater industries of our nation we see great change in the employer-employee relationships. We see changes in the status of women, in family patterns, in attitudes toward authority, in scientific discoveries, and on and on.

Most of us have come to realize that we live in an evolving world and that change is the very essence of things. The problem for most of us is when change comes into our lives. It is hard to think of anything about us becoming different, but changes do come, and when they come, many of us feel defeated. We want to keep things as they always have been, but children have a way of growing up and leaving home.

As we grow older, we assume different positions in society: a husband or a wife can die; a divorce can take place or our jobs can be radically changed.

Instead of a defensive attitude toward change, we need to let the gospel of hope speak with a powerful voice as changes occur. Let us quit linking together the words "change" and "decay." Let us think of some other words instead of "decay" – such as, "better," "more interesting," "new," "challenge," "hope," and on and on. If a change comes into your life, it is not necessarily a defeat.

Neither society nor a person can grow without change. Sometimes changes involve suffering, tragedy, and even failure, but change also can mean victory and joy and achievement. Change has the power to almost dehumanize persons, but it also has the power to enlarge us, and make us better.

In her book *Let Love Come Last*, Taylor Caldwell put it this way:

> "Can you imagine how impossible the Constitution would be if we didn't continually add amendments? Amendments are signs that the Constitution is in a healthy state, and growing constantly. Whenever a man or nation changes its opinions, or enlarges them, he or it hasn't as yet died."

On the other hand, when changes come into our lives, let us remember to hold fast to the important values that make life worth living. Let us remember to save the old that is worth saving. It is a thrilling thing to walk through a great art museum and see there the works of the masters of previous generations. Even though we enjoy seeing new art forms, we can continue to cherish the masterpieces of the past. The furniture in our homes, for the most part, is different from that of past times. Yet many people continue to cherish some antique piece of furniture. It is more valuable now that when it was first created.

It is the same in our lives and in our characters. Our situations do change. Life is not the same, but there are certain human and spiritual values which we hold fast.

In the midst of change, one of the strengthening and uplifting exercises we can engage in is listing the things in our lives that we think are important enough to hold on to – no matter what happens. Holding onto these changeless values gives us strength when we need it the most.

Bloom Where You're Planted

A fine young man came to see me recently with a problem that is almost universal. When he was young he dreamed of a specific career, but circumstances barred him from the job on which his heart was set. Now he is disappointed and feels cheated. He wanted to be a doctor, but he did not have the money necessary for his education and had to quit school and go to war. Now his chance to be a doctor is gone and he is filled with regret. There are a lot of people who are not able to do the things their hearts were once set on doing.

When I fly to Washington and pass over Mount Vernon I always think of George Washington. The city below, that he planned, is our nation's capitol. Millions of people see the great Washington monument and give thanks for such a man. But George Washington wanted to be a sailor in the King's navy; that was the dream and ambition of his early manhood. His trunks were packed and his ticket bought to sail for England. However, at the last moment his plans were changed and he did not go. His disappointment was almost unbearable, but out of his disappointment came a far greater life.

When our government issued a commemorative stamp in honor of mothers, the painting *Whistler's Mother* was chosen. Whistler was the greatest portrait painter of his age, though, as a young man, he wanted to be a soldier. He went to West Point and flunked. Then he tried engineering and failed. As a last resort he took up painting and became famous.

When I think of Jean Francois Millet I am grateful that once a man lived who could paint such pictures as "The Angelus," "The Reapers," and "Man with the Hoe." The picture that gave Millet his chance was "Oedipus Unbound." But the picture he worked hardest on was his "St. Jerome," and it was rejected by critics.

Millet was so poor that he could not afford to buy more canvas for a new picture, and he was so disappointed that he felt like quitting. But he did not quit. Instead, he took his rejected canvas and over it he painted his first successful picture. His disappointment became the base for his success.

One of the ambitions of my own life was to serve as a Roman Catholic priest. I did for 15 years and am thankful for the lessons I learned. My life took a different course when I married the love of my life and began working for non-profit organizations such as hospice. I would not go back and change things now, even if I could.

All of us experience disappointments, some more than others. Our hearts are set on certain goals and we find ourselves unable to carry out those fond dreams and ambitions. Instead of foolish regrets, we must take advantage of the opportunities that come our way. Instead of whining and feeling sorry for ourselves, we must find something positive to do. We must bloom where we're planted.

The Turning Point

Published after his death, Dag Hammarskjold's private diary inspired many people. He made one statement which especially inspired me. He said, "I don't know WHO – or WHAT – put the question. I don't even know when it was put. I don't even remember answering, but at some moment I did answer YES to SOMEONE or SOMETHING – and from that hour I was certain that existence is meaningful, and that therefore my life has a goal."

There are in all people marvelous possibilities – if they will just believe, commit themselves, and work at it. I am thinking now about a man who was born in a simple, rural community. He had few life opportunities and little chance for education. The material possessions of his family were meager. As a little boy, he dreamed of being a preacher. Often he would stand in a chair and preach to an imaginary congregation. He had a natural gift for singing, and though he never had an opportunity to study music, he became a member of the choir in a monastery. As a young man he joined the church.

He had a good mind. When he was eleven years old he made all "A's" in school, and the other pupils naturally looked up to him as their leader. One of the things he enjoyed was reading the books of James Fenimore Cooper, and he delighted in acting out those marvelous stories.

He loved great music, and it is said that he heard Wagner's "Lohengrin" ten times in succession. He reached the point where he could whistle long passages from operas and would entertain his friends. He became a reader of history and philosophy and also found strong interests in art and architecture.

A tragedy came into his life when he was 14 years old. His father died and he became the "man of the family." When he was seventeen years old he went to live in a city. He had a small inheritance which he received from his father, so

The Gentle Art of Caring

he had time to visit art museums, attend opera, read, and think. When he was with a group of friends, he always was the center of attention because of his ability to impersonate great characters.

He had only been in the city one year when his mother became critically ill. He hurried home and devoted himself entirely to caring for her. When she died, he was grief stricken for many weeks and even months. He would not accept the inheritance his mother left him, so he gave it to a sister. To another sister he gave an inheritance from an aunt.

Later, his country declared war on some other countries, and he volunteered for the army. He was a good soldier and was decorated for bravery.

While he was in the army, a little dog ran into the trench where he was sitting. He caught the little dog, began to pet it and feed it, and they became friends. Later, someone stole the little dog, and for days this man was almost beside himself with grief.

Once he found some hungry mice and regularly fed them bread crumbs. He seemed not to want to hurt anything or anybody.

He especially loved people who had never had an opportunity in life. Once a poor man gave him two eggs, and he was deeply moved with gratitude. He loved children and he would make colorful and beautiful kites for the youngsters of the community. One day a little boy bumped his head against a chair and began to cry. To show his loving sympathy, this man beat his own head against the chair. Then, for the sake of the little boy, he spanked the chair.

When he got out of the army he was 29 years old. He wanted to serve his nation in some way. He seemed to have no personal ambitions; he just wanted to give and help people. When he was 34 years old he wrote a beautiful poem about his mother in which he pleaded with people to love their own mothers.

We ask the question: Who was this man? We are really surprised when we learn that his name was Adolph Hitler. I think we would all agree that he became probably the most destructive and diabolical personality in all of history. This man, who loved people, killed millions and caused untold suffering.

Every person has an equal capacity for good or for evil. The greatest saint has the ability to be the most evil, and the most evil person has the ability to be the most saintly. Whatever our inner capacity is, it can go in either direction. As we grow older, we either become bitter or better.

What Are You Going To Do?

Some people think harmlessness is holiness. They think the only requirement for goodness is not being bad. They take great pride in the sins they do not commit, and they are satisfied because of the harm they are not doing.

If you are looking for a happier and richer life, make a list of "What-am-I-going-to-do?" questions and get started. Try this positive approach and see how much better it works than a negative approach.

Ask yourself these four questions:

1. **What are you going to do this month to make yourself a better person?** What will you do? Speak kindly to every person you meet? What are you going to do?

2. **What are you going to do this month to make your home happier?** One person might say family prayers; others might say they would clean up their yards and make them look better. What are you going to do?

3. **What are you going to do this month to make your church or an organization you belong to better?** People might list such things as regular attendance, inviting others, contributing more, etc. What are you going to do?

4. **What are you going to do this month to help your community?** You could work for better recreational facilities for youth or strive for community cooperation. What are you going to do?

If you want to experience the joy and thrill of positive living, ask and answer the "What-are-you-going-to-do?" questions. By the end of the year you will experience a total change of attitude.

Gardening may interest you. You can select a plot of ground, dig up every weed, and get the plot as clean as a highway. But you never will have a garden until you get some flowers or vegetables growing there. We need to remember that the value of a rose bush is measured, not by the number of thorns it does not have, but rather by the number of roses it does have.

For some time I felt an impulse to bake a cake. I had never baked one, but the recipes seemed so simple that I wanted to prove to my wife how easy cooking really is. So I took the cookbook down and selected a recipe that suited me, chose the proper pans and ingredients, and went to work. Some three hours later I sadly realized that baking a cake requires a wonderful talent, one that I certainly did not seem to possess.

There are many other talents. Cheerfulness is a talent. It is good to be able to write a poem, but it is better to be able to live a poem. Some people are born with a talent to be happy and to make others feel happy.

One of the finest talents is the ability to be a friend. To be able to overlook faults in others, to center into the sorrows and joys of others with a sympathetic heart and to be loyal and true no matter what happens. When we hear the word "talent" we usually think of the ability to play a piano, make a speech, sing a song, or to be brilliant at something else. But the far more important talents are in certain qualities of character that mean so much to the people around us.

This is a great big world, and there are so many ways I can spend my life. In fact, there are so many ways I would like to spend it, it is hard to know just what to do. I can spend it all just for myself.

One of the unexplainable but true mysteries of life is that you never lose what you give. No person every really begins to live until he finds something big enough to give himself to. The very best and biggest way I can invest the life I have is to give it back to others who gave it to me. In that way I am sure to get more out of it. It is true for all of us. What are you going to do with your life this month?

A Maturity Check Up

How many times have you played golf with someone who missed a shot, got mad, and for that reason missed the next shot too? There is nothing sillier than having a temper tantrum on the golf course just because you didn't hit the perfect shot. What is needed is relaxation and self-control.

We have heard people say, "I have a temper," as if that is something to be proud of. Every person has a temper, but not every person knows the art of self-control. We have the power to master our emotions so that we are always in control.

For one who has had to learn the fine art of self-control the hard way, I have four suggestions:

1. **Determine your most vulnerable point.** I know people who can endure prolonged pain yet go to pieces under a criticism.

Impatience is the problem of many. Some cannot stand it if everything doesn't go his or her way. At that point, we need to consider our prejudices. The list could be extended as to why people get upset, but the important thing is for each of us to determine our own Achilles heel.

2. **Try to understand other people.** If we know a person, it is much easier to take a loving attitude.

Suppose some person is rude to you. It may be a clerk in a store, or someone you work with, or an inconsiderate automobile driver, or one of your neighbors, or one of your children, or your wife or your husband. Instead of becoming irritated or angry, ask the question: "I wonder why that person acts that way?" That question could have various answers. Maybe that person is sick, or has experienced a deep sorrow, or has been mistreated by someone else, or any number of reasons.

3. **Try to understand your own emotions.** When you feel yourself getting upset, try to understand why. This can lead to most helpful self-examination.

Epictetus said, "Reckon the days in which you have been angry. I used to be angry every day; then every other day; then every third and fourth day; and if you miss it so long as thirty days, offer a sacrifice of thanksgiving to God."

4. **Develop companionship with God.** Realize that you are in the presence of a higher being.

A friend of mine told me that he easily becomes frustrated on the golf course and, after a bad shot, will use loud profanity. He said he is noted on the links for his behavior that certainly lacks self-control. He said there is one person he enjoys playing with most of all because he never loses his temper or expresses a word of profanity and inspires my friend to do the same. That person is his minister.

Suppose one realized that he or she is in God's presence, or the minister's presence, or a notable person's presence. What a marvelous difference that would make!

One of life's temptations is to wear our feelings "on our sleeve." In some strange way, getting our feelings hurt feeds our ego. To forgive or forget a wrong toward us is in a sense to surrender. It is our natural inclination to fight back.

It is so easy to keep account of wrongs against us, to be too sensitive, to look for evil when none was intended. But love almost refuses to be insulted or to be hurt. There is a toughness and a strength about love that protects one's heart and feelings, like a suit of armor protects the body. Try the following **"Maturity Check-Up"**:

1. Mature people do not take themselves too seriously.
2. Mature people keep their minds alert.
3. Mature people do not always view every adverse situation that arises with alarm.
4. Mature people are too big to be little.

The Gentle Art of Caring

5. Mature people have faith in themselves which becomes stronger as it is fortified by faith in a Higher Power.
6. Mature people never feel too great to do the little things and never too proud to do the humble things.
7. Mature people never accept either success or failure in themselves as permanent.
8. Mature people never accept any moods as permanent.
9. Mature people are able to control their impulses.
10. Mature people are not afraid to make mistakes.

You can be what you want to be if you learn and apply the right principles for your life.

The Gentle Art of Caring

PART SIX – MINDSETS WE LIVE BY

Critical or Complimentary

We can be critical or complimentary, and in our speaking we reveal our true selves. We can spend our time saying the world is beautiful, life is good. Somehow it turns out that way. On the other hand, we can spend our time complaining and being critical, and our very speech drags us down.

Speaking of being critical, I was in a restaurant one evening, and I enjoyed overhearing the following conversation:

A man was drinking his coffee and said to the waitress, "This coffee is terrible. It tastes like kerosene oil. Is it tea or coffee?" The waitress replied, "If it tastes like kerosene oil, it's coffee. Our tea tastes like turpentine."

The point is, you can get in the habit of being critical, and everything you touch or taste becomes bad. Not only am I a person who can talk. I am also a person who can think. Being able to think, I can make decisions. Being able to make decisions gives me the power "to become," but it also gives me the power to become "undone." Who am I? A lot of it depends on what I decide to be: critical or complimentary.

We can bring about good in our lives if we use our four dimensions – length, breadth, depth and height.

1. **Length.** In response to the question, "How long do you want to live?" I can always answer, "As long as I can." Or if someone asks me, "Are you prepared to die?" I always reply, "Not if I can help it." One dimension of life is length, and most people want to live in that dimension.

2. **Breadth.** We need the dimension of breadth. A broad person understands and sympathizes with the people

on this earth. There are many differences between people. However three things remain the same the world over: a smile, a tear, and a drop of blood. These three things represent our most important emotions. When we come to know each other and understand each other, then we find ourselves concerned with each other.

There are three philosophies of life: First, what belongs to my neighbor belongs to me, and I will take it. Second, what belongs to me is mine, and I will keep it. Third, what belongs to me belongs to my neighbor, and I will share it. Someone expressed three philosophies of life in these words: "Beat 'em up, pass 'em up, pick 'em up."

Living in the dimension of breadth, one is concerned about others.

3. **Depth.** Depth is the third life dimension. If you plan to build a tall building, first, you dig down to form a strong foundation. Unless one has certain convictions about life, sooner or later that person topples and falls. Faith, friends, reputation, education, and skills – all of these form foundations for living.

4. **Height.** In height we find dreams, our hopes, our goals, our ambitions, and our ideals. The phrase "Hitch your wagon to a star" is good advice. Once someone asked a mountain climber how he maintained his strength in climbing the mountain. His reply was, "I keep looking up."

Living the four dimensions makes us compliment everyday realities. We discover ourselves and deliver ourselves to others. Our life is dedicated.

Guilt – The Big "G"

Sooner or later every person experiences what we call the Big "G" – Guilt. We look back and remember wrong decisions that we made, harsh words that we spoke, places where we failed, opportunities we did not seize, sins we committed and goodness we did not develop. To some degree, every one of us has a past we are ashamed of and feel guilty about. Our past has a way of staying with us, influencing our lives, bringing sadness to our hearts, making it harder for us to get on with the business of living.

We need to realize we cannot escape our past. Whatever it is, good or bad, that's what it is. Of course, there are many happy things in our past we don't want to eliminate. It's also true that every saint has a past, every sinner has a future.

There is some guilt which we must face and deal with or it becomes dark shadows over the remainder of our lives. I cannot count the times I have heard laments such as, "Why didn't I call the doctor sooner?" or "Why did I say those mean things that were so unnecessary?" or "Why did I do what I did?"

However, let's not dismiss the value of remorse. It can be cleansing and a positive experience in our lives. Thinking about past wrongs and mistakes brings us an inner restlessness. Thoughts of the past can destroy all peace of mind in the present. Self-reproach and shame just don't go far enough, but remorse can lead us in the right direction.

There are three steps that must be taken when one feels remorse: penitence, pardon and peace. The first we do ourselves, the second we accept for ourselves, the third is an unmerited reward. When we repent for some past wrong, it is the best that is within us crying out for fulfillment. It means that we turn away from that which we regret. Dante wrote, "He who repents not, cannot be absolved. Nor is it possible to repent and at the same time to will to sin, the contradiction not permitting it."

Don't be sad that you feel sorry about something in the past. Be glad that you feel sorry. William L Sullivan put it beautifully, "There is in repentance this beautiful mystery – that we may fly fastest home on a broken wing."

The inability to repent is probably the worst imprisonment that any person can experience. The ability to repent means that there is the possibility of freedom, to turn "about face," to change your mind and, most importantly, to start a new life.

There is an old story of a man who stopped at a country store to ask the distance to another town. The reply was, "If you continue in the direction you are going, it will be about 25,000 miles, but if you turn around, it will be about three miles." Repentance means the freedom to turn around. That is glorious and wonderful. Most importantly, repentance leads to forgiveness.

An Attitude of Gratitude

The secret of happiness is an attitude of gratitude. As Brother David Stendle-Rast says in his book *Gratefulness: The Heart of Prayer*, "In daily life, we must see that it is not happiness that makes us grateful, but gratefulness that makes us happy." This depth of gratitude arises from an overflowing heart. We are grateful for the very fact of being alive. Children are far better at this than we grown-ups are. We can learn much about gratitude by watching how excited and joyful children become and try to incorporate those feelings into our daily lives.

Saying "Thank you" is something we do every day, usually automatically, to strangers and loved ones alike. I am amazed that when I say "Thank you," consciously and from the heart, it changes my day. I have seen how total strangers will respond differently to my words of thanks when I speak to them consciously, with real meaning.

I am inspired by grateful people. A priest friend of mine has a habit of sending out one thank you note a day to honor good behavior. A restaurant owner has a unique tradition of giving gifts on his birthday instead of receiving them. A donor who I was thanking for a recent gift turned the tables on me by stating, "No, don't you thank me. I thank you for giving me the opportunity to give to your non-profit."

As a fundraiser for various non-profits over the years, I understand how important it is to thank donors between three and seven times. People need to be appreciated for the good they do. And when you say thanks to others it has a positive effect on the one giving thanks.

Once you take the philosophical stance that everything is a gift, then no matter what happens, you will look for the positive lesson, outcome, or potential inherent in any situation you face. It's your looking for the gift that makes each experience a gift.

You need an attitude of gratitude adjustment if you consistently exhibit any of the following behavior:

- You whine and complain a lot and often contribute a negative comment about any topic.
- You frequently feel like a victim.
- You haven't enjoyed a sunrise or a sunset in the last few years.
- You have trouble getting started in the morning.
- You have trouble enjoying the present moment.
- You have resentment about events in the past.

This inner decision of gratitude is not at all related to a Pollyanna philosophy. It's not a blind sort of optimism. It's really a deep, spiritual decision of how you want to relate to life. It's a mindset. I want my attitude toward life to be independent of the inevitable ups and downs. I want my philosophical stance to be consistent, not reactive to other people, circumstances, or luck.

Years ago I scribbled down this short verse which I refer to regularly:

> "With feet to take me where I'd go,
> With eyes to see the sunset's glow,
> With ears to hear what I would know,
> Oh, God, forgive me when I whine;
> I'm blessed, indeed! The world is mine."
> -Anonymous

Forget About It

By her voice over the telephone I surmised that she was a very cultured woman about 60 years old. Extremely careful not to reveal her name or anything about herself that would allow me to guess her identity, she obviously was very upset and needed help.

She told me that her children thought she was a good woman, but there was something on her conscience that had worried her for many years and she could no longer stand it. She said it was something she had done as a young woman. More than anything else, she said she wanted peace – a peace of mind and heart – but that with this thing on her conscience she could not have it. She called me to ask what she could do about it.

Ordinarily, when people talk to me about past wrongs, I never let them tell me too much. In the first place, I have heard about everything that one might be guilty of, and in the second place, often people will reveal things when they are upset that later they will regret revealing. But in this instance, because I did not know the person, I felt it might be helpful to know exactly what she had done that was worrying her. So I asked for the details and she told me that as a young lady she worked in a store. One day she took a little change out of the cash register, meaning later to replace it. A few days later she took some more, then for about a year she continued to take small amounts of money.

It seemed harmless at the time. It was a big store and could afford to lose the money, especially because she felt that they were not paying her as much as she was worth. You cannot justify a wrong, even to your own conscience.

This dear lady got my sympathy. Imagine her carrying such a burden in her heart for probably 40 years. At night she could not sleep because of her guilt. Many times she missed all the beauty of this wonderful world about her because her mind was darkened by something ugly. Her quality of life was ruined when it would have been so easy to straighten out and make peace within her heart.

Gladly I told her what to do. I hope she did it and will enjoy peace of mind and heart during the rest of her life. First, she needed to make restitution as best she could. It would be all right to anonymously send to the store what money she could afford. Then, just for the asking, she could have the pardon of God. And, finally, she needed to pardon herself. To get her own forgiveness would be the hardest for her, and I suggested some ways to go about it.

One of the greatest steps for a happy life is to learn how to forget. As a counselor I have talked to a number of people who have had nervous breakdowns. For the most part, they "broke down" because they were trying to carry too heavy a load. In a majority of cases that load was an accumulation of past mistakes and failures.

George Herbert said that when an individual undresses for sleep at night, that person should also undress the soul from the day's mistakes and failures. All people make mistakes. Successful people are those who have learned to say to themselves, "Forget about it!"

Be The Boss of Your Habits

One can say, "We live by our habits." When we are standing still and start to walk, we almost always put one particular foot forward. Some start on the left foot, some on the right, but it's almost always the same foot for each person. We constantly perform acts unconsciously. We walk, we eat, and we do so much of what we do by habit without thinking about it.

In reference to habit, each of us can fit into one of four categories. Briefly, let us look at these:

1. **There are people who have the habit of never attempting anything that is difficult.** They have no heart, except for the easy task. They are interested only in merely getting by in life. They give as little as they possibly can. Yet the same people wonder why others make progress, while they are held back.

2. **Next are people who never hear what anybody else has to say.** They never try to learn; they never observe; they are the "know-it-alls." It is always a disagreeable experience to be in the presence of a person who never hears any part of the conversation, except what he or she has to say.

3. **Another group of people are those we call "the fighters."** They are against everybody and everything. They never see good in others or in any institutions. In their thinking, the government is bad; the schools do not teach; the people who go to church are hypocrites and on and on. They express their hostility at every opportunity. Someone has called such people "vicious wet blankets."

4. **There is a fourth kind of person who has developed the habit of looking for good in other people.** One who is willing to do more than is expected, who has developed the qualities of a lady or a gentleman, who never puts people down, but is

seeking to lift people up. This person is interested in making everything in the world better than it is. The glorious thing is that in lifting others up, this person is lifted up.

The greatest accomplishment in life is the mastering of oneself, and there is no deeper joy than to realize that we are living life at its very best. In reference to any enslaving habits, we need to face the question, "Who's the boss?" The realization that we are improving brings self-confidence, maturity, strength and happiness.

When Trouble Comes

Sooner or later every person faces some kind of trouble. There are many types: illness, financial reversals, job frustrations, marital problems, some hurt that comes to one of the children, an unhappy relationship between parent and child, unrealized ambitions that are never realized, and many other troubles.

No one promised us a life without trials or skies always filled with sun. We need to remember six very important truths about "trouble experiences."

1. When we are troubled, **we must remember our need for each other.** At a funeral service for a lovely mother I was deeply impressed as the four children stayed so close to their father and to each other. At this time of great sorrow there was a real need. In times of illness it means a lot to know that somebody cares. In fact, in the latter years of life, having the realization that somebody loves you is one of the most stimulating experiences of life.

2. In times of trouble and danger, **we are more aware of the uncertainties of life and even of the uncertainty of life itself.** To begin with, knowing that life is uncertain, we must make added effort to enjoy the good and happy times we experience. In the second place, even though we are going through difficult times, there always is the possibility of something good happening. Through the years I have taken many trips in airplanes. Often you find yourself in a cloud, and it is always a sense of joy and relief when the plane breaks through the cloud into the bright sunshine. So it can be with the experiences of life. We are not sure when we will be in the sunshine and when we will be in the clouds, and so we are prepared for the uncertainties.

3. Times of trouble, whether they are illness or sorrow, are not times for problem solving. In these times, there is a tendency to think of all of the difficulties and problems of life which just makes everything worse. **Wait until the storm passes and then solve your problems.** Illness throws us off balance emotionally. In times of trouble we have a tendency to lose our poise and equilibrium. Little things become big things when life is not going well. When we are hurting it is much easier for our imaginations to get out of hand. A sleepless night can seem like an eternity. We can get to the place where we do not think clearly, and things get blown out of proportion. In times of trouble do not let your mind become absorbed with all the other troubles of life.

4. All through the Bible we are promised dividends from our troubles. Trials and tribulations might be gold mines from which are taken some of life's richest prizes. Through the years I have visited with many people experiencing serious problems. If our trouble is illness, it often gives us an opportunity to be quiet, to think, to more properly evaluate life, to develop sympathy for other people, to learn that the world can keep going no matter what happens. During times of trouble **we develop a realization of the higher purposes of life**, and there is a tendency to lose some of our selfish independence and be thankful for our dependence upon other people. During trouble we become aware of and thankful for the achievements of medical science.

5. More importantly, in times of trouble and especially illness, we become sure of God. Once there was a woman who was trying to turn the light on in a telephone booth. A passerby said, "Lady, if you will shut the door, the light will come on." Many times when troubles come and we shut the door, **the light**

does come on. Ralph Waldo Emerson said, "A person is a hero, not because that individual is braver than anyone else, but because that person is braver for ten minutes longer."

6. Not all troubles turn out well, not all sick people get well, not all of life's hurts heal. One of the greatest comedians the world has ever known was Sir Harry Lauder. When he heard the news that his son had been killed, he said:

> "In a time like this there are three courses open to a man. He may give way to despair, sour upon the world, and become a grouch. He may endeavor to drown his sorrows in drink or by a life of waywardness and wickedness. He may turn to God. **It may be that he cannot overcome the pain but he can find the power to endure it.**"

Sarah Williams wrote a poem called, "The Old Astronomer." In that poem are these lines:

> " Though my soul may set in darkness
> It will rise in perfect light,
> I have loved the stars too fondly
> To be fearful of the night."

Judge Not

Why are we so quick to judge others? Let me note here five reasons why we pass judgment upon others:

1. **Being conscious of our own sins, we take comfort in someone else's faults.** There are two ways to boost ourselves. One way is to live up to the highest and best of that which we are capable; the other way is to pull the other person down to our lowest level. The latter way is much easier. This is the reason why people like to repeat gossip, in comparison, it makes them feel better.

2. **We judge others because we are jealous.** Often it is that secretly, in our hearts, we would like to be committing the same sin we condemn. We suspect that the other person is having more fun than we are. But we do not do as they do because we lack the nerve, or the opportunity, or our own conscience won't let us. Still, we resent the other person doing these things. Often it is the thing we most condemn that is our greatest desire or temptation.

3. **We judge others because we do not know all the facts and circumstances of their lives.** Surely it is that so many times we do not know what another person is doing. The ancient Rabbi Hillel said, "Do not judge a man until you yourself have come into his circumstances or situation." We cannot know the strength of another person's temptation.

4. **Judging others takes our minds off our own sins.** It is a lot more comfortable to talk about the mistakes and wrongs of another's life than it is to face up to the wrongs of our own lives.

5. **We judge others quickly and harshly because we lack love in our hearts.** When we love others, we will live the truth of this little verse:

"Don't look for the faults as you go
through life,
And even when you find them,
It's wise and kind to be somewhat blind,
And look for the virtues behind them."

-Anonymous

There are two important reasons why we should be very careful in our judgments:

1. **We do not know all of the facts, therefore, we cannot judge fairly and impartially.** According to the records, the Greeks held a particularly important and difficult trial in the dark so that the judge and jury could not see the man on trial; they did not want them to be influenced by anything but the facts in the case. The truth is that our judgments are clouded and influenced by so many things, and it is almost impossible for us to look at another life and give an unbiased verdict. Our judgments can be so wrong.

John Wesley tells of a man whom he had condemned for many years. Wesley felt that the man was one of the stingiest people he had ever known. He knew that the man had a handsome income, yet he contributed very little of it. On one occasion when the man gave a very small gift to one of Wesley's causes, Wesley criticized the man very caustically. The man looked Wesley in the eye and said, "I know a man who, at the week's beginning, goes to market and buys a few cents worth of parsnips, and takes them home to boil in water, and all that week he has parsnips for his meat and the water for his drink, and meat and drink alike cost him a few cents a week." "Who is the man?" asked Wesley, "I am," was the reply.

Later, Wesley wrote these comments in his journal: "This he constantly did, although he then had an adequate income, in order that he might pay a debt he had contracted long before he joined my congregation. And this was the man that I thought to be covetous."

2. **The second reason we should not judge others is that we are not good enough.** Before we express judgment against others, let's be sure that our judgment passes the threefold test:
   a. Is it true?
   b. Is it necessary?
   c. Is it kind?

And let us never forget a little poem that most of us have known since childhood:

> "There is so much good in the worst of us,
> And so much bad in the best of us,
> That it hardly behooves any of us
> To talk about the rest of us."
>
> -Anonymous

Indecision

I am sure that indecision is one of the most harmful experiences in any person's life. I still remember an experience I had as a little boy. Several of us were playing by the side of Beargrass Creek. We were talking about whether or not any one of us could jump over the creek. I looked at the creek and said I believed I could do it and the other boys dared me to try. I got back a distance, so as to get a good running start. As I was getting close to the creek, however, it looked wider and wider, and I began to have some doubt that I could do it. I started to jump at the same time I felt that I ought to have held back. The result was that I landed in the middle of the creek. I got all wet and my friends laughed at me. If I had resolutely made up my mind to jump the creek, I believe I could have done it. My indecision squandered my power.

One of the most tragic plane accidents I ever heard of took place at Bowman Field years ago. A friend who was at the airport and saw it told me that the plane started down the runway. It was gathering speed but not as fast as it should have. After the plane got a considerable distance down the runway, the pilot decided he would try to stop it, but he was going too fast to stop and the result was a crash in which a life was lost. My friend who witnessed the accident said that he believed that if the pilot had kept his motors open and continued to go on, he would have gathered enough speed to take off safely. The crash came because of his indecision.

I remember a cartoon I saw of a picture of a donkey standing between two haystacks. The donkey was hungry and the aroma of the hay was appetizing. He looked toward one haystack and start; then he would think of the other haystack, and look back, and start toward it. The end of the cartoon was that the poor donkey starved to death, standing between the two fragrant haystacks, simply because he never could make up his mind.

This was the trouble with Hamlet. Hamlet did not have the ability to act, and so he said, "To be, or not to be, that is the question." He never could decide.

It is said that when Robert Louis Stevenson had an important decision to make, he wrote in one column all of the reasons why he should do that certain thing. Then, in another column, he wrote down all the reasons why he should not do it. He then compared the two columns and made his decision. The great misfortune of so many people today is that they never really face up to life's important decisions.

One of my great loves is baseball. To be a great hitter in baseball one does not have to get a hit every time one bats. In fact, a player can fail two out of every three times and still make any baseball team in America. But to me the most disappointing sight in a game is to see a player stand with his bat on his shoulder and let the third strike be called on him. To swing and miss is not so bad, but to stand there and not do anything is terrible.

So it is in life. Every decision one makes does not have to be the right one; even the wisest will make mistakes. But if you ever expect to succeed, you have got to be willing to make some decisions, to take some chances and go on. To stand through life with your bat on your shoulder is to fail in the worst way.

We were not free to choose the day and generation in which we were born, our heredity, or even the color of our skin. Some are born with a talent to sing, others with a talent to work with their hands. But we all are free to use our opportunities or let them slip by, to double our talents or bury them in the weeds.

I am free to be good or bad, to fill my life with hate or with love, to live for self or to live for service, to make the world better or worse, to count for something or to count for nothing.

SECTION SEVEN
THE "HOW-TO" SECTION

How to Start Yourself

So often we concentrate on "How To Stop Something You Want To Stop." But it is better to know "How To Start Something You Want To Start." Let us consider four simple steps for starting yourself:

1. **Fix clearly in mind what it is you want to start.** Someone has well said that the world turns aside and gets out of the way of people who know where they are going. You can't expect to get anywhere if you do not know where you want to go.

2. **Get started.** It is good to call to mind that old story of how the devil wanted to destroy the world. He called his chief assistants. First came Anger who said, "Let me go and destroy humankind. I will set brother against brother, sister against sister. I will get people so angry with one another and they will destroy themselves."

Next spoke Lust, "I will defile people's minds. I will make love disappear and turn men and women into beasts." Then Greed said, "Allow me to go and I will instill in people's hearts the most destructive of all passions. Uncontrolled desires will destroy them all."

The twins, Gluttony and Drunkenness, came and told him they could make people's bodies diseased and dysfunctional. Envy, Jealousy and Hate each told how they could destroy everyone. Idleness claimed to be equally effective.

But with none of these was the devil satisfied. Finally, the last assistant came in. This one said, "I shall talk to people persuasively in terms of all that God calls them to be. I shall tell them how fine their plans are to be honest, clean and brave. I shall encourage them in the good purposes of their lives."

The devil was aghast at such talk. But the assistant continued, "However, I shall tell them there is no hurry. They can do all of those things tomorrow. I shall advise them to wait until conditions become more favorable before they start."

The devil replied, "You are the one who shall go on earth to destroy humankind." It was Procrastination – just put it off a while longer. Get started. NOW spelled backward is WON.

3. **Believe you are going to succeed.** One of the most dramatic sports events of all time was when Babe Ruth pointed to the fence in a World Series game in Chicago and then drove the ball over it for a home run.

After the game a reporter said to Babe Ruth, "Suppose you had missed that final strike?" A look of surprise came over Babe's face, and he said, "Why, I never thought of that."

A lot of people start with doubts and thoughts of failure in their minds, and they fail almost every time. Nothing will dissipate your power faster than to think failure.

It is simply amazing what people can do if they keep believing and trying. Often, however, that is not easy. The human mind will resist struggle. It will want to give up in surrender. It will seek the dead peace of hopelessness. To keep believing positively is difficult, but it is the pathway to power and victory.

4. **Rely on a power greater than yourself.** Remember, the God who created electricity did not forget to create a power for us that would pull us over life's steep hills. When, with humility of spirit, we go into partnership with God, a new and thrilling power comes surging in.

I love the saying, "Be careful what you set your heart on, for you will surely get it." Know exactly what it is you want to start. Then plant deeply and persistently in your thinking this phrase, "All things are possible."

How to Stop Something

How do we stop something that needs to stop. Everybody is interested in this because at some point nearly every person has something that needs to be stopped. It may be a habit, such as gambling, drinking, smoking, or profanity. It may be some mental habit, such as self-pity, jealousy, worry, or fear of failure.

There are four simple steps which, if carefully and persistently taken, will free us of any habit of action or thinking which enslaves us:

1. **Decide exactly what it is you need to stop.** That is not always simple or easy. For example, a man told me he needed to stop being critical of other people. But the cause of his critical attitude was jealousy. Underneath his jealousy was a very real feeling of inferiority. The reason for that was the fact that he was lazy. What he needed to stop was being lazy.

There are vast numbers who need to stop drinking. That may involve a special process which Alcoholics Anonymous is using in a superb manner. But many drinkers are not alcoholics. They drink because of the crowd they associate with, or because they are trying to escape from something. Maybe it is because they have not found a satisfying outlet for expression, or maybe they are unwilling to put forth the effort that living requires and find that alcohol is a simple substitute.

2. **You must decide whether or not you really want to stop.** One of the profound truths of psychology is that whatever you really want done probably will be done. The reason that we often have difficulty in stopping something is that our minds are divided. One part of the mind says, "I ought to stop this." The other part of the mind says, "I like this, and I don't

want to stop it." And that mental division squanders one's decision power.

3. **The next step is simply to make up your mind to stop.** Just quit acting like a baby. Don't sit around whining and whimpering, complaining and excusing. If you are going to quit, go ahead and quit. Just do it.

4. **Believe harder.** This is the most important step. The first three steps are not enough. They would be enough if each one of us possessed a resolute, undefeatable, iron will. But we don't have that. By using your will power you say you will stop. But your imagination, which is stronger than your will power, tells you that it's too hard. When you admit your own weakness and fill your imagination with belief, marvelous power begins to flow in to support your will. Then nothing can defeat you. You plant indelibly in your mind these words: "I can do it. I believe."

One of the most profound truths of psychology is that whatever you want to do you probably will do. One of the deepest truths of spirituality is that with the help of your higher power, nothing can defeat you.

How to Get Along With Others

Andrew Carnegie paid Charles Schwab a salary of a million dollars a year. Why was he willing to pay a man more than three thousand dollars a working day? Was it because Mr. Schwab knew more about steel than any other man? No, under him were many individuals who knew more about steel and its production. He drew that salary because he knew one fundamental and most important thing -- he knew how to get along with other people. If you know that one thing there is hardly any limit to the possibilities of your success in any area of life.

Any person who wants to be happy and successful must learn how to get along with others. Here are some simple rules that work for all who try them. They are not original with me. I have read a lot along this line, have observed many successful people, and these seem to be the fundamental rules:

1. **Get interested in other people.** You can win more friends in a month by being interested in them than in ten years by trying to get them interested in you.

2. **Don't criticize anybody about anything.** When you criticize people, they immediately set up a defense mechanism against you.

3. **Do your work and forget about who gets the credit.** Give the other folks credit and they will love you with a passion.

4. **Greet criticism from others with a smile and good will.** No person can continue to hold a grudge against you unless that grudge is at least partly returned.

5. **Learn to get along with yourself.** More often than not, conflicts between ourselves and others spring from a conflict within ourselves.

6. **Remember the law of projection and the law of extension.** The law of projection means that the faults we see in others mirror the faults we see in ourselves.

The Gentle Art of Caring

The law of extension means that the love we see in others mirrors the love we know within ourselves.

The ability to get along with others, is, to my mind, the most precious talent any person can possess. It will do more for you than anything I know. Remember the words of William James: "The greatest revolution of our generation is the discovery that human beings, by changing the inner attitudes of their minds, can change other aspects of their lives."

How to Get What You Want

"Is there a something, a force, a factor, a power, a science – call it what you will – which a few people understand and use to overcome their difficulties and achieve outstanding success?" Claude M. Bristol asked that question and he answers it by saying, "Yes." He calls that something "The Magic of Believing."

That is, when you picture something clearly in your mind and entirely give yourself to it, you can do even seemingly impossible things.

When you decide clearly and definitely what you want, then no sacrifice is too great as you put all of your powers into astounding results. Get perfectly relaxed and quiet in an attitude of prayer, and conceive of your mind as a blank motion picture screen.

Then flash on that screen the picture of the thing you want to accomplish. Look at the picture, then take it off. Then flash the picture back. Repeat that process, perhaps over a period of days, weeks or months, until every detail of it is clear and sharp.

If there is something you want, do not be afraid to ask for it. However, there are four principles we must observe:

1. **Decide exactly what you want before you ask.** Then test your desire. Is it good for you? Are you ready for it now? Is it fair to all others concerned? Do you honestly feel it is according to your Higher Power's will? If you can say yes to those four questions, then do not hesitate.

2. **Ask for it.** Take the positive approach, knowing that no matter how hopeless it seems there always is a way. I read about a man who hit on a wonderful idea. Every night when he went to bed he would put his keys in one of his shoes. The next morning when he put on his shoes, his foot would hit those keys. He would take

them out, and say this little prayer: "Lord, I know there is a key to every situation. May I not give up this day until I find the keys I need."

3. **Do what you can to answer your own requests.** A woman in an office asked for a raise. Her boss explained that she was being paid the top salary for a clerk, but if she would take evening classes and increase her computer and office skills she would be in line for a fine increase in pay. But she was not willing to do that. She asked, but was not willing to help herself.

4. **Ask, believing.** When we believe, then our prayer is already answered in our minds. Maybe not actually in our lives, but our prayer has come within the realm of possibility.

One may say that these are the three steps to success: (a) "visualize," (b) "prayerize," and (c) "actionize."

The first step is to visualize clearly the things we really want. Then "prayerize." In its deepest meaning, prayer is not asking for something, rather it is committing our lives to our Higher Power.

A man once told me that he wanted some things and was bitterly disappointed. He said that my "theories" did not work. I said, "I want to ask you two questions:

"First, what are you doing with what you do have?" There are two principles involved in that question. One, it is possible to think so much of what we want that we forget what we have. It often happens that most of our wishes do come to pass and we fail to recognize that fact.

For example, I asked this man what his greatest desires were 20 years ago. He said he wanted a wife, a home with children, and a job to support them. I asked if his wish came true, and he said it did. I suggested that instead of being bitter about some disappointments, he might, instead, be thankful for the great desires of his heart.

I then asked him, "Is your life committed to your Higher Power?" A completely dedicated life develops abilities and strengths that one never possessed before.

The third step is "actionize," that is, willingness to do all you can. The second oldest college in America is William and Mary in Williamsburg, Virginia. Today it is one of our most honored institutions. However, in 1881, as a result of the financial catastrophe which resulted from the War Between the States, William and Mary closed.

It probably would have remained closed but for the faith of its president, Dr. Benjamin Ewell. Every morning for seven years he rang the old college bell. That is about all he could do, but he did that. And one great day William and Mary reopened.

Visualize – "Prayerize" – "Actionize," and your wishes will come true.

How to Stay Young

Ponce de Leon was not the only one who sought the fountain of perpetual youth. In one way or another each of us seeks that fountain. We do not like to think about losing our strengths, being wrong and even fainting. We do not want to get old; we think of old age as calamity.

I love the story of how one day, when John Quincy Adams was 80 years old, a friend greeted him on a street in Boston, "Good morning, Mr. Adams, how are you today?" Then came the youthful answer, "Mr. Adams is quite all right, thank you. Of course, the house he lives in is a bit dilapidated; its walls are tottering on their foundation; its roof is greatly in need of repair. I think he is soon going to have to move out of his old house into another not made with hands. However, Mr. Adams is quite all right. Thank you."

While thinking of the marks of old age, there are some ways to stay young. Let us consider three ways to avoid the loss of our youth:

1. **Face the fact that there is no way to stop bodily aging.** Certainly, proper health care and sane and sensible living habits help our bodies to stay younger longer. However, there is nothing we can do to stop life's clock. We cannot avoid old age by tearing up the old family record, by refusing to admit our ages, or resenting the fact that we are not as young as we used to be.

In fact, we ought to be very grateful that we are growing older. Suppose the process was reversed: Instead of growing older, we would be shrinking younger. If I got younger instead of older, it would be the most horrible thing that could happen in my life. As the years shrunk up, you would lose each one of your grandchildren and then each one of your children and all the good and happy experiences you have accumulated all these years. I would not give up one year of my life.

2. **To avoid old age, we must be interested in the life of today.** Nothing is more withering and deadening than loss of interest. There are those in their 20's who are fed up. They face life without enthusiasm or joy. Maybe there is a lot of wrong in the world today, but this is our day and it belongs to us, and it is the only day we have. It is exciting to think about tomorrow.

Ask yourself the question: "What excites me most about the future?" If I were answering that question I could write many things, but I think the one that excites me the most is the thought that someday we will be able to be in communication with human beings on some other planet. It may be that there is civilization on another planet far more advanced than our civilization, and what a glorious thing it would be to be in contact. It really might happen. But if that doesn't happen, I know that many wonderful things will happen, and I want to live as long as I can and see as many of those things as possible.

3. **As long as we keep crawling, we are not old.** Luigi Pirandello wrote a fascinating play called *Six Characters in Search of an Author* performed at a local regional theater several years ago. They are in search of an author who will bring them to life in an actual presentation and include them in the journey.

Once a man who was going through a very difficult experience said, "I have reached the place I cannot walk, but I can crawl, and I want you to know I have not stopped." We are still on the journey.

The Gentle Art of Caring

How to Sleep at Night

If you could look at this man who came to see me, you would think that he never had a worry in his life. Big, strong, manly, successful in business, he owns a nice home; he has a lovely family, and is highly respected by his friends. I was surprised when he told me he was sick, and I suggested that he see his physician.

But he had already been and after a number of tests and examinations, his physician told him he was in perfect physical health. When he kept insisting that something was wrong with him, the physician had suggested that he talk with me.

I asked him his trouble. It was that he could not sleep at night. He told me he had not had a full night's sleep in six months.

I named a current book on how to sleep that is selling well. He already read the book and it did not help him. I asked about his bad habits but he seemed to have a lot fewer than I have, so I dropped that approach. I asked about his conscience but he assured me he had done nothing that was disturbing him.

I told him that he was not alone in his problems, that every night ten million Americans took a "sleeping tablet," but he said he had taken so many that even those no longer helped him.

We continued talking, and finally he said, "I have everything a person should want in life, but I am just plain scared and I don't know why I am scared."

I took a sheet of paper and wrote across the top of it these two words, "Still Waters." I handed him the sheet of paper and told him to put it in his pocket and before he went to bed that night to write down under the quotation everything he thought it meant and whatever related thoughts it brought to mind. Then I asked him to put the paper in his dresser drawer. The following night he was to take out what he wrote, read it over, and add whatever thoughts had come to him. He was to keep that up every night for a week and then come back to see me.

I wanted to saturate his mind completely with that one thought. I know that it is utterly impossible to simultaneously keep fear and thoughts of "still waters" in one's mind. Any good fisherman can testify to that. That is the reason that fishing is such a great medicine for so many people.

There is no nerve medicine on this earth that can compare with still waters. When we create those clear, cool, still waters on the screen of our imagination, it is wonder-working. As Longfellow put it, "Sit in reverie, and watch the changing color of the waves that break upon the idle seashore of the mind."

Well, I wish I could say that this man came back the next week refreshed, relaxed, and at perfect peace. But, to tell the truth, he did not come back at all. He felt he was too big and important for such a simple little exercise. He wanted me to tell him something complicated and mysterious, and when I told him such a seemingly simple thing to do, he was disappointed.

"Still waters" – Sweet peaceful sleep comes easy to any person whose mind is saturated with that one thought. Of course, no medicine ever works for those who will not take it, and one must take the entire prescription.

PART EIGHT – SPIRITUALITY: GROW A SOUL

Live Large – Grow A Soul

We are always concerned about the growth and development of our physical bodies. But many times we neglect to realize that we each have a spiritual self. If we are to experience the high joys of life, we must nourish and develop our spiritual selves. As someone put it, "Every person must grow a soul."

Three women go to a great concert. The first one is a musician to her fingertips. She knows, understands and loves the music. She traces with delight every repetition of the theme through all the variations of an intricate figure. The second woman has not the musical soul of the first woman, but she enjoys it as much as she can. Her limited capacity limits her enjoyment of the music. The third woman is completely bored. She secretly longs for the end. To her it is punishment to sit there.

To some degree that is the way people experience the business of living. We fail to "grow our souls" because we do not use our spiritual capacities. They lie dormant within us. The fish in Mammoth Cave have eyes, but they cannot see. They live in darkness through generations and, without use, their eyes become sightless. So it is with any of our faculties. Quit praying, and one gets to the point where prayer becomes difficult indeed.

In our spiritual growth, we may easily develop a false optimism that prevents immediate effort. Some day we plan to consider our spiritual natures, but we are too busy now with other things.

More tragically some people remain satisfied with the state they are in. They dream no dreams. They feel no more call of the Spirit of God. They are not stirred by the impulses of their hearts.

The great sculptor Bertel Thorvaldsen noticed the waning of his power when he stood before a statue he had just completed and he felt dissatisfied. The tragedy was that his hand had caught up with his dreams.

It is a fact of life that when we become dissatisfied and feel the need for something beyond our own strength, somehow there is a power which literally reaches to us and picks us up. Whatever our weakness, there is a strength available to us which is more than enough to overcome that weakness.

Sometimes people say that they have never had this feeling of divine presence. Once a lady stood watching Jim W. Turner, a great artist, as he painted a glorious sunset. She commented, "But Mr. Turner, I never see any sunsets like yours." "But Madame," he replied, "Don't you wish you could?"

When we hear of people feeling God's presence, there is a longing in our hearts for that same experience. At times it would be worth more than anything on this earth, and I can say to every one of us that it is possible as we give spiritual things their proper place in our lives.

The Quiet Rhythm of the Universe

I believe Blaise Pascal's quote, "All the troubles of life come upon us because we refuse to sit quietly for a while each day in our rooms."

Every day I take at least ten to thirty minutes to quiet myself and meditate. This is more important to me than constant activity. It brings me inner peace, self-confidence, and optimum results.

More than any other clergy, Dr. Norman Vincent Peale inspires us. I remember him telling a story about a lady who finally just broke down under the strain of life: the daily pressure, her worries and fears, her hurts and disappointments. She went to the beach to spend a few days, just to rest quietly. One day, sitting out on the beach, her body was in such a position that she became conscious of the beating of her own pulse. She noticed there was a definite rhythm in her pulse which fascinated her.

As she felt the rhythm within her own body, she happened to notice the tall beach grass all around her which had been washed clean by the tide. A gentle breeze blew the grass back and forth, back and forth, back and forth. To her astonishment, she realized that the moving of the sea breeze also had a rhythm – a rhythm very much akin to the rhythm within her own body.

She lifted her eyes and began to watch the rise and fall of the sea. She saw the waves slowly coming in across white sand. To her astonishment, she realized the rise and fall of the water of the mighty ocean also followed a rhythm. It was the same rhythm that the grass had and that she had felt within herself.

Suddenly she caught the point: a human being, the beach grass, the mighty ocean are all part of one creation. As she lay on the beach, she realized that the power within the universe also worked within her.   She felt her strength renewed.

Too many times our hearts are ruled by turmoil instead of peace.   Enrico Caruso, the great singer of yesteryear, held a very fragile glass between his thumb and forefinger. He sang an ascending scale, holding a high note, and suddenly the glass would shatter into pieces under the vibration.

That same thing can happen to people.   High frequency nervous tension can wreak havoc on human personalities and bodies.   There is no way of escaping the vicissitudes of human existence.

Robert Louis Stevenson said it this way, "Quiet minds cannot be perplexed or frightened but go on in fortune or in misfortune at their own private pace like the ticking of a clock during a thunderstorm."   That is a beautiful analogy. No matter how hard the wind blows or how loud the thunder crashes, the clock does not change its pace. It keeps its same steady tick tock, tick tock, tick tock.

When we find ourselves attuned to the quiet rhythm of the universe, we find renewed strength.

Things I'd Like to See

There are many things I have had the joy of seeing in my lifetime – the Grand Canyon, Hawaii, some of the great cathedrals of Europe, the isle of Capri, and the Canadian Rockies. There are many things I still want to see – the Holy Land, Australia and New Zealand, the Greek isles, Germany, and Victoria Falls. I want to continue to see my home happy and peaceful. I want to see the difference between right and wrong. Most of all, I want to see my Higher Power.

Of all our physical faculties, we probably most cherish sight. We would rather lose our hearing, or our ability to speak, or even our arms or legs than to lose our sight. To help us to see more we use the microscope and the telescope. We spend millions and millions on motion pictures, and television is one of our largest industries. We like to see and we sympathize with one who is blind. Once I saw a blind man on the corner with his tin cup that stopped nearly every passerby. About his neck was a sign reading, "It is May and I am blind."

But not all people have the same ability to see. Many people have limited vision. Some are cross-eyed, the eyes of some are weak and diseased. Some people have a growth called a cataract, which shuts off vision. Some are near-sighted; others, far-sighted; some are color-blind; others have blind spots in their eyes. Sidney Lanier looked at the muddy, crooked Chattahoochee River and saw in it a lovely poem; Joel Chandler Harris saw it in rabbits, foxes, possums, and an old man named Uncle Remus, stories which will live forever. Woodrow Wilson saw a basis for lasting world peace, but, tragically, so few others saw it. Sir Christopher Wren could see a beautiful cathedral and make of that vision a temple of God.

There are at least three ways in which we see. There is the sight of the natural eye, with which we can see flowers and mountains, the printed words on this page, and people's faces. That is physical vision.

A teacher may explain to a boy a problem in math or chemistry. As the teacher talks, the boy hears, and his mind takes hold of what he hears to the point of understanding. After he understands, he may say, "I see it." That is mental sight. In studying botany a student can reach the point of learning the various kinds of flowers and of their culture and development. Then he can see flowers with both his physical and mental eyes. If one understands what he reads, he sees with both his eyes and his mind.

But there is still a third sight. The heart has eyes too. Robert Burns saw in flowers thoughts too deep for tears. Not only did he see flowers with his physical eyes, not only did he understand the growth and culture of flowers, but he also felt their message. A man can look at a woman and know that he loves her. He sees her not only with his eyes but with his heart.

Often people who live alone have more time to be quiet and to think. We need to set aside moments to make an effort to be aware – to begin to understand in our minds what our ears listen to – to see with understanding what our eyes behold – to begin to respond to the stimulations of life which are all around us – and to get the message from every situation.

Awareness means that we begin to realize something of the infinite potentiality that is within even ourselves. Beyond that, awareness is a deep sensing of other persons. I think Anne Morrow Lindbergh said it well in these words, "Each person is an island, but all are connected by a common sea. We therefore are aware of the potentiality of the person, but are not limited by our own limitations." Henry Miller said it equally well, "It's good to be just plain happy; it's a little better to know that you're happy; but to understand that you're happy and to know why and how and still be happy, be happy in the being and the knowing, well that is beyond happiness, that is bliss."

The Path of Acceptance

A few years ago the parents of a friend of mine got the heartbreaking news that their son, Greg, was going blind, and that nothing could be done. Everyone was torn with pity for them, but they remained calm and uncomplaining. One night, as I left their home, I tried to express my admiration for their courage.

I remember how Greg's father looked at the stars. "Well," he said, "It seems to me that we have three choices. We can curse life for doing this to us and look for some way to express our grief and rage. Or we can grit our teeth and endure it. Or we can accept it. The first alternative is useless. The second alternative is exhausting. The third is the only way to follow – the path of acceptance.

The path of acceptance – how often that method is rejected by people who refuse to admit their limitations, who hide behind lies, who react to trouble with bitterness. And how often when one makes the first painful move toward repairing a damaged relationship, or even a broken life, that move involves acceptance of some thorny and difficult reality that one must face before the rebuilding can begin.

It's a law that seems to run like a shining thread through the whole tapestry of life. Take alcoholism, for instance – that grim and mysterious disease. Where does recovery begin? It begins with acceptance of the unacceptable, with the uncompromising four words with which members of Alcoholics Anonymous introduce themselves at meetings: "I am an alcoholic."

Or take a failing marriage – a marriage that is on the rocks, or drifting toward them. Any marriage counselor will tell you that no reconciliation ever succeeds unless it involves acceptance of the other partner, faults and all, as an imperfect being. And acceptance, too, of the fact that the blame for the trouble must be shared.

The Gentle Art of Caring

Difficult? It's terribly difficult. But in terms of courage and cheerfulness and ultimate happiness, the rewards can be beyond measure. I knew a priest once, who through some hereditary affliction was deaf and almost blind. He went right on preaching, visiting the sick, listening to people with his hearing aid, laughing at jokes, sharing huge portions of himself with others and having a marvelous time.

One Christmas I went with him to buy some odds and ends in a crowded drugstore. On the back of the entrance door was a mirror, so placed that as we turned to leave, father's reflection came forward to meet him. Thinking that someone else was approaching, he stepped aside. So, naturally, did the image. He moved forward and once more met himself. Again he retreated.

By now an uneasy hush had fallen on the spectators. No one quite knew what to say or do. But on his third advance father realized that he was facing a mirror. "Why," he cried, "It's only me!" He made a grand bow. "Good to see you, old boy! Merry Christmas!" The whole store exploded in delighted laughter, and I heard someone murmur, "That man really has what it takes." What "it" was, surely, was the gift of acceptance – the acceptance of limitations that in turn brought the power to transcend them.

There was no apathy in the acceptance of the parents of my friend Greg who lost his sight. They helped him learn Braille. They convinced him that a life could be useful and happy even though it had to be lived in darkness. He's doing great in college now, and his attitude seems to be a cheerful, "My handicap's blindness. What's yours?"

In such cases, acceptance frees people by breaking the chains of self-pity. Once you accept the blow and the disappointment, you're free – free to go on to new endeavors that may turn out magnificently.

Perhaps in the long run the beginning of wisdom lies in the simple admission that things are not always the way we would like them to be, that we ourselves are not so good or so kind or so hard-working as we want to believe. And yet . . . and yet . . . with each sun that rises there is a new day, a new challenge, a new opportunity for doing better.

"Oh Lord," goes one version of the old prayer, "Grant me the strength to change things that need changing, the courage to accept things that cannot be changed, and the wisdom to know the difference." People call it the prayer of acceptance. They are right.

And It Came To Pass

Some time ago I attended the funeral service for a teenage girl. Later the mother said to me, "How long will it take to get over this sorrow?" I replied, "Do you really ever want to get over it?" She quietly answered, "No."

We do not "get over" our sorrows. Sorrows become permanent and precious possessions of our lives. Unfortunately, sorrows have the power to make us either bitter or better.

I have many times felt myself in the situation of a little girl whose mother sent her on an errand. When the little girl returned late, her mother asked why. She explained that a playmate of hers broke a doll. She stopped to help her. The mother wondered how she could fix the little girl's doll. She asked, "How did you help her?" Her reply is truly wonderful. The little girl said, "I sat down and helped her cry." Time and again I have not been able to help the situation. The only thing I could do was sit down with somebody and help them cry.

An argument could be made that the word "why" is the greatest enemy of humankind. Again and again we are moved to say "Why?" There are some people, however, who reach the point of discovering that life is to be enjoyed and not explained.

Instead of asking why we lose something, we should begin to take inventory of what we have left. There is still some life in you. There are deeds to be done. There are people we can love. There are things we can enjoy. Plant firmly in your mind that you can keep going, no matter what happens, that you have not lost everything, and life goes on.

I go back to the thought of our worst enemy: the word "Why." The more we think about it, the more we might be able to say, "Why not?" Instead of saying, "Why me?" let us get to the place where we can honestly say, "Why not me?" The question "Why not me?" may bring the very wonderful results of overcoming in your mind and life the mystery of trouble and grief, and in its stead, give you the power of love and redemption.

Some time ago I talked with a very distinguished retired minister. He told me that he was 87 years old, and ever since he learned to read he has read at least one chapter of the Bible every day. Most days he read several chapters. He has read entirely through the Bible a number of times. I asked him, "Having spent so much time reading the Scriptures, what is the one verse that you would pick out as your favorite?"

I could hardly wait to hear his answer. Here was a man who had lived more than eighty years with the Bible, who knew it, as the saying goes, "from cover to cover." He hesitated about replying. Finally he said to me, "You will find my favorite Bible verse fifteen or twenty times, scattered through the Bible." He said, "And it came to pass . . ." (Exodus 12:41, Acts 27:44, and many other places).

I really was shocked and disappointed. I said, "Do you mean to tell me that in all the Bible that one dangling phrase, 'And it came to pass,' is your favorite verse?"

And when he answered me, I felt like I was being rebuked. "Let me tell you that there is no verse in the Bible that can help you more than this." He went on, "I have lived long enough to know the truth to that phrase, 'It came to pass.' All the miseries of life come to pass. Even the joys of life come to pass. All the heartaches, the troubles, the wars, the crime – all come to pass.

A baby is born in your home, but the baby grows up and becomes a man or woman. It came to pass. You have your job, your work in life, but it came to pass. You marry and live with someone whom you love more than you love yourself – but it came to pass."

I started thinking about some of the happenings in my own life that I worried about – some of the events that I felt were very hurtful and that maybe I would not get over. Now, as I look back, I realize, "It came to pass." I thought about some of the occurrences that I thought were of the utmost importance, but now they are not important at all. They "came to pass."

This also applies to so many delightful and pleasurable experiences. We need to learn how to enjoy what we have when we have them, because all of the pleasures of life eventually "come to pass."

If today you feel heavy burdens and heartache, if you feel tomorrow is hopeless, if you feel that you do not have the resources, the strengths to make it in life, just remember, "It came to pass." Nothing came to stay. Tomorrow will be a new day with a new chance, new strengths, and new opportunity. If you can really believe, "It came to pass," then all despair in your life can somehow be taken away.

Celebrate the Dignity of Living Everyday

So many people feel insignificant, unworthy, and unimportant. The truth of the matter is: there are no unimportant people and no unimportant events. A man sat in the shade of a tree and saw an apple fall and discovered the law of gravity. His name was Isaac Newton. Another man sat in the kitchen and saw a teakettle steam. It was a significant experience because, seeing that teakettle, he discovered the principle of the steam engine. His name was Robert Fulton. There are no insignificant people or insignificant events.

Somewhere I read the story of a Boston landlady who interviewed a prospective tenant. To impress her, he took his wallet out of his pocket and showed her its contents. She replied, "Do not show me your wallet; show me your beliefs." She is completely right. The most important thing about a person is not how much money that person has or how many honors that person received; the most important element is what a person believes.

Study the people who are really popular with other people. You will find several common traits among them. To begin with, popular people are those who are interested in others. They treat them with respect and courtesy. They are quick to both appreciate and to encourage, and they are very slow to criticize.

In contrast there are many people who belittle people. In belittling others we belittle ourselves. Let me list some the ways we depreciate others:

- Often we make uncomplimentary remarks about other persons. When we hear something unkind about another person, let us ask ourselves three questions: Is it true? Is it necessary to repeat it? Is it the loving thing to repeat it?

- In conversation with others, do we complain about the circumstances of our lives? Self-pity is self-depreciating. On the other hand, genuine pity for the circumstances of the other person is a marvelous quality. We depreciate ourselves through self-pity. We exalt ourselves through unselfish pity.

- Do we make accusations against others, or do we listen to accusations of others? Really there is very little difference in making an accusation and in hearing an accusation. We should refuse to hear belittling things about our friends. People who listen to gossip belittle themselves.

- One of the things we need to be careful about is feeling that we need to constantly explain our actions. That indicates a lack of self-confidence, a lack of self-respect. On the other hand, instead of feeling the need to explain (which shows lack of confidence), one might go to the opposite extreme in loud and excessive boastfulness.

More especially we need to be slow to criticize ourselves. We have made mistakes, we have failed, but we need to remind ourselves that mistakes can be corrected – that failure need not be final.

Walt Disney applied at the <u>Kansas City Star</u> for a job as an artist. He was told that he did not have talent and was urged to give up art. His first cartoon, "Oswald the Rabbit," was a total failure, but after that he drew Mickey Mouse.

In thinking about ourselves, let's remember that greatness comes not "of whom we were born," but "for whom we were born." Greatness comes as we see something to give ourselves to and for. Whoever we are, we can lose our lives in some great cause and celebrate the dignity of living.

Every so often I find people who have "lost faith." Not having faith in life, it becomes stale and insipid. No person is perfect, but every person can live a better life. Every person is of supreme worth. Instead of condemning ourselves for what we are, we should dream of what we might become. Faith in the dignity of life believes in the impossible. One of my favorite stories about the impossible comes from the pen of Lewis Carroll:

"I can't believe that!" said Alice.
"Can't you?" the queen said in a pitying tone.
"Try again: draw a long breath and shut your
eyes." Alice laughed. "There's no use
trying." She said: "one can't believe
impossible things."

Amazing and wonderful things begin to happen as we believe in ourselves and celebrate the dignity of living every day. Stand in reverent respect before that which inspires you. Feel new strength and power; then, in the name of the highest and the holiest, get going.

PRESENTATIONS AND PRODUCTS

♥ ♥

Bob Mueller's presentations are tailored to meet your organizations needs.   Topics include:

- Positive Living
- Stress Management
- Motivation
- Personal Growth
- Spirituality

To schedule a speaking engagement, please contact Bob at LookForwardHope@aol.com or write to:

> Positively Speaking Enterprises
> 3902 Keal Run Way
> Louisville, KY   40241-3031
> Or call (502) 640-7810

Books

Look Forward Hopefully - $14.95

Sensible, heartening and inspired advice on how to live more fully and calmly in the troubled world that is ours. Each of these reflections points out directions for those who are crowding life's road seeking light and truth. Topics include:

- Why We Worry
- Enthusiasm Reaches Goals
- Principles to Live By
- Twelve Steps to Peace

"By far and away, the most popular column we have in the News-Leader is "Positively Speaking" written by Bob Mueller. Unlike other . . . columnists whose purpose is to make people think, laugh or get mad, Mueller writes to make us feel good about ourselves. His columns uplift the human spirit inside each of us and speak to our heart and soul. Any reader who takes a few minutes to read Mueller's column finds his/her spirit and attitude has changed for the better. *Look Forward Hopefully* . . . contains columns that are among the best of his practical inspirations."

"Mueller is a calm, patient counselor reaching out and embracing you. His writing style makes it feel it was written just for you. No lecturing, just a warm and new perspective to address your worry."

"*Look Forward Hopefully* belongs on a must read list of any person who needs good, simple, inspiration for peace and fulfillment."

– *The Reporters, Inc. News-Leader*

Book Order Form

Title	Qty
☐ **Look Forward Hopefully**	_____
☐ **The Gentle Art of Caring**	_____

Order Quantity _____

X $ __14.95__

Order Total .... $ _____

Kentucky Residents add 6% sales tax .... $ _____

Shipping & Handling - $2.00 per Book .... $ _____

Total $ _____

Please make check payable to PSE Publishing.

Mail Order Form to:

PSE Publishing
3902 Keal Run Way
Louisville, KY 40241-3031

The Gentle Art of Caring